BROADWAY PLAY PUBLISHING, INC.

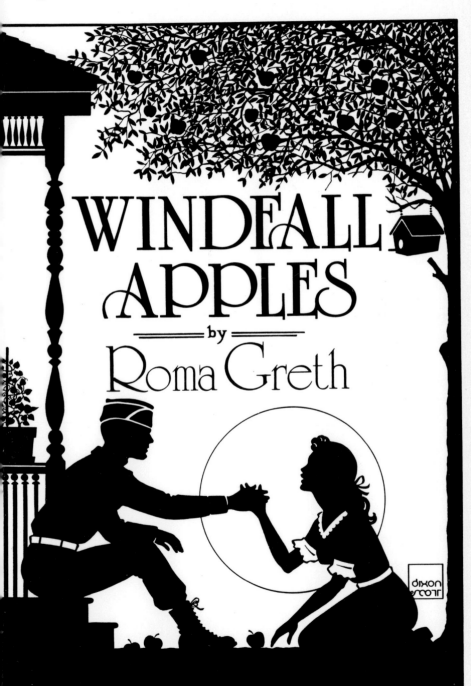

WINDFALL APPLES

by

Roma Greth

BROADWAY PLAY PUBLISHING, INC.

WINDFALL APPLES

by

Roma Greth

249 WEST 29 STREET NEW YORK NY 10001 (212) 563-3820

WINDFALL APPLES

First printing: June 1984

ISBN: 0-88145-018-9

Cover Art by Dixon Scott
Design by Marie Donovan
Set in Baskerville by L&F Technical Composition, Lakeland, FL
Printed and bound by BookCrafters, Inc., Chelsea, MI

WINDFALL APPLES was originally presented at the O'Neill Center in a staged reading in 1977. It opened at the Impossible Ragtime Theatre on December 8, 1978. The creative elements of the IRT production were as follows:

TONY	John Del Regno
WALLY	Patrick Desmond
MARTIN	Ron Jacobson
JUNE	Lily Knight
LORRAINE	Charmain Sorbello
DANIELLE	Adrienne Wallace

The director was Anita Khanzadian. The costumes were designed by Sheryl R. Barenboim; the lights, by Terry Bennet; the sets, by Terry Noble.

CAST

June Eisenhart, ungainly girl of about 16
Lorraine Eisenhart, her mother, living in another world
Wally Eisenhart, her father, well-dressed, socially inclined
Danielle Silverman, her friend, 16, popular girl
Martin, Danielle's cousin, a soldier, good-looking, sensitive, about 21
Tony, another soldier, common man, same age as Martin

SETTING

Interior and exterior of the Eisenhart home at the edge of a small city in Pennsylvania

TIME

Early November 1943

ACT ONE

*The scene is an old suburban area outside of a small city in Penn-
sylvania the weekend before Armistice Day in 1943. This is a single
set showing a room, part of a front porch, and a portion of the yard of
the Eisenhart home. The room is raised about two feet above the stage.
It is furnished with overstuffed furniture of the late 1930s. Tidies are
on chair backs and arms. An upright piano is covered with a fringed
shawl and holds family photographs: skinny girls grinning shyly,
beautiful young women in picture hats, and soldiers of many wars.
Above the sofa is a long picture in faded brown which shows the entire
company of a World War I Army unit. Imitation oriental design rugs
are on the floor. Many vases filled with paper flowers are about. There
is a door which leads to a kitchen; an open stairs leads upward. Since
it has been a warm season, reed chairs are still on the porch. A flag
holder is attached to the railing. In the yard is an old, gnarled apple
tree, leafed with rusty green; on the grass beneath are apples which
have been brought down by the wind. Enclosed by the picket fence
which shuts off the street beyond are other apple trees, perhaps felt,
rather than seen. The time is early on a Saturday morning. Light has a
pale look as if the shortening days are neglecting sunrise as they move
toward solstice.*

It is quite dark in the house as JUNE EISENHART *comes down the
stairs. She wears pajamas and a robe which she is just fastening about
herself. The clothing are as plain as she is. She goes to the front door
and opens it just as the rays of the rising sun come spreckled through
the old tree. She raises her arms to the sun, making an oval of them.
Leaving the door open she goes to a table where a small candle has been
placed. She lights the candle, then goes to the piano bench and rum-
mages beneath sheet music to find a deck of playing cards. She seats
herself before the candle and lays out a reading. It must be established
that what she is doing is, to her, an occult ritual. Then, upstairs a
man coughs and makes other morning sounds.* JUNE *is surprised at an
interruption this early on a weekend morning and for a moment sits
frozen. Then she quickly blows out the candle, gathers up the cards,
closes the front door quietly, and ducks into the kitchen. She*

is just in time as WALLY EISENHART *comes down the stairs. He is nattily dressed and appears to be pleased with his world. He carries small rolled-up flags, and a small but neat suitcase.* WALLY *breathes a spirit of health and life. He checks himself in the living-room mirror, is pleased with what he sees, and goes outside. The day is becoming brighter. He pauses on the porch to sniff the air. It meets with his approval. With something of ceremony he puts the flags into the flag holder, making sure they hang properly. He is still working on them when the phone rings inside the house. He rushes inside to grab the phone.*

WALLY: Hello? (*Almost a whisper.*) My God, I told you not to call me here again! Just a minute. (*He puts down the phone, goes to look upstairs and listen carefully. He tiptoes back to the phone and continues to speak in a low voice.*) Margey? . . . Are you still drunk? (*Chuckling.*) Yeah, we had a swell time last night, but, Marge, you know how it is here. Suppose one of them had picked up the phone? . . . You devil—she's been telling me about these calls she gets where there's nothing but heavy breathing. . . . You bet it's going to be a swell weekend. But do you know what time of day it is? How'd you know I'd be up? (*Laughing.*) I know I'm good but I didn't know I was that good. . . . The diner? *Now?* . . . You're nuts, honeybunch, you know that? . . . Who's complaining? I love it, Margey, I love it. I need somebody like you. . . . Okay, see you in fifteen minutes. But, Margey— for Christ's sake, don't call me here!

(*He hangs up with some exasperation. But his thoughts of the woman on the other end take over and, grinning at her audacity, he jauntily straightens his tie, picks up his suitcase, and leaves the house. The moment the front door closes behind him,* JUNE *comes out of the kitchen with a glass of orange juice. She hurries to the window and watches as* WALLY, *whistling, crosses the yard and exits. There is the sound of an automobile starting up somewhere on the street and pulling away.* JUNE *looks at the phone and thinks about the conversation she has obviously overheard. Still pondering, she goes to the piano, finds comfort in touching the keys, then sits and begins to play an angry classical tune.*)

LORRAINE: (*From upstairs.*) June!

JUNE: Yah?

LORRAINE: (*Off.*) What time is it?

JUNE: Uh—about eight.

LORRAINE: That's War Time. Real time it's only seven—
what're you doing up so early Saturday morning?

(JUNE *continues to play. In another second* LORRAINE EISENHART
appears on the stairs. She is a faded woman who looks years older than
WALLY, *although they are both in their forties. Her hair and clothing
are ten years behind the style. She is putting an old flannel robe over a
well-worn nightie.*)

JUNE! Stop that! You know your father's going away this
weekend!

JUNE: He's already up.

LORRAINE: What?

JUNE: And out.

LORRAINE: Oh.

JUNE: He's always up early.

LORRAINE: Not this early. Not Saturdays.

JUNE: Maybe the diner's crowded on Saturdays.

LORRAINE: I don't know why he thinks he always has to
have breakfast in that dirty diner as if . . . (LORRAINE *goes to
the front door, opens it, and stands looking out as though she expects to
see him there.* JUNE *stops playing.*) . . . Seems Indian summer's
going to hang on until December this year.

JUNE: Wish he'd take me along.

LORRAINE: What?

JUNE: I think it's fun to eat breakfast out.

LORRAINE: It's a waste.

JUNE: Rich people always eat breakfast in restaurants.

LORRAINE: Oh, June. I don't know where you get some of
your ideas.

(LORRAINE *goes outside;* JUNE *follows.*)

JUNE: Dad's rich.

LORRAINE: Rich!

JUNE: The shop's got war contracts.

LORRAINE: For a few thousand parachute cans. That's not going to make us rich.

JUNE: Well, he's eating breakfast at the diner every morning since he got the order.

LORRAINE: "A fool and his money . . ."

JUNE: Why don't you ever go along?

LORRAINE: Waste of gas dragging down there and back. You'd think we had a C-ration instead of A the way he acts. (*At flags.*) He's already put the flags out for Armistice Day.

JUNE: Uh huh.

LORRAINE: Look at all these apples the wind brought down. Early frost and windfall apples. . . . What's that a sign of? It's either a bad winter or a good one. (*She picks up a few apples from the ground.*) I'd better make applesauce this after.

JUNE: I don't like applesauce.

LORRAINE: I'll bet you ate applesauce for your grandmother when you lived with her on the farm.

JUNE: Maybe.

LORRAINE: No wonder she liked you better than she ever liked me.

JUNE: Didn't you eat applesauce for her when you were a kid?

LORRAINE: Yes, but I liked it.

JUNE: In Grandmom DuBois' house you didn't dare not to.

LORRAINE: She was a strong woman. Crops just seemed to come up out of the ground because she willed it. (*Sadly inspecting some bedraggled, frosted plants.*) Too bad the Victory garden didn't do better.

JUNE: Too much shade from the trees.

LORRAINE: More like not enough elbow grease from your father. (LORRAINE *makes a sling of her robe and picks up more apples.*)

JUNE: Mother . . .

LORRAINE: Um?

JUNE: (*Watching her reaction to this carefully.*) Danielle's parents sleep in the same room.

LORRAINE: Jewish people are more—sensuous than we are.

JUNE: Yah?

LORRAINE: Look at all the begatting they did in the Old Testament.

JUNE: Even the kids in school that aren't Jewish have parents that sleep in the same bed.

LORRAINE: You taking a census?

JUNE: Everybody thought it was funny that you and Dad had separate rooms.

LORRAINE: June DuBois Eisenhart! Where I sleep is my business.

JUNE: I told them President and Mrs. Roosevelt have different rooms. And they have five children.

LORRAINE: You're going to graduate from high school next spring. When are you going to grow up?

JUNE: Maybe I don't want to grow up.

LORRAINE: Most girls your age are just dying to grow up—do things—get married.

JUNE: I don't think getting married is doing much.

LORRAINE: Good as anything else, I guess. It all ends up six feet under anyhow. (LORRAINE *has picked up a rotten apple which she squeezes until the juice and soft pulp run over her hand to drip to the ground.*) Decays. The soft parts, even the ones men think so much of. Go into the earth. Rot. Nothing left except juice—to feed the roots of the trees.

JUNE: (*Takes a handkerchief from the pocket of her robe and cleans her mother's hand.*) *Mother!*—What's the matter?

LORRAINE: Nothing.

JUNE: You're down in the dumps again.

LORRAINE: Wise child. You know your parents. It's your tragedy.

JUNE: I didn't hear you and Dad fighting lately.

LORRAINE: We don't fight! We—discuss.

JUNE: I didn't hear you and Dad discussing lately.

LORRAINE: . . . I feel so sorry for these apples.

JUNE: You feel sorry for everything.

LORRAINE: (*Nodding as she realizes the truth of that.*) I even miss the parts of my body they took out when I was in the hospital.

JUNE: Mother, you were sick. They had to take out your uterus and that other stuff.

LORRAINE: Don't call it that!

JUNE: In hygiene class that's what they—

LORRAINE: I bet they just threw it away.

JUNE: What else do you expect them to do with a—whatever?

LORRAINE: I'd have buried them. Here. Under the trees. That's the place to bury things.

JUNE: Oh, Mother—

LORRAINE: They'd have fed the trees. My womb—somehow —it would have changed—into—(*She holds out an apple.*)

JUNE: No wonder I don't like applesauce.

LORRAINE: (*Staring at apple.*) Become alive again.

JUNE: Mother, where's Dad going this weekend?

LORRAINE: What?—Oh. It's that thing with the Vets.

JUNE: What thing?

LORRAINE: If you and your father would talk to each other once in a while—

JUNE: Every time we talk it turns into a—discussion.

LORRAINE: It's that Shrine. I think that's what they're calling it, though seems to me there should be less-Catholic words for such things. Memorial! That's it. The Memorial they put up to his machine gun battallion. He showed me a picture—big thing like a tombstone on end. They're dedicating it this weekend.

JUNE: All weekend?

LORRAINE: Oh, it's going to be a big time.

JUNE: How are they going?

LORRAINE: Train. And probably taking up some soldier boys' seats, too.

JUNE: Mother—why don't you go with him?

LORRAINE: Me?

JUNE: Yeah. Why not?

LORRAINE: Oh, no, I—

JUNE: Boy, I hope you're not going to tell me that you don't go places like that.

LORRAINE: I don't! Any place you have all those vets, you have—drinking. Smoking. And worse.

JUNE: You wouldn't have to drink. Or smoke. I don't know about worse.

LORRAINE: You mind your tongue, girl!—I'm going to climb the wooden hill.

JUNE: No, don't go back to bed! Go with Dad.

LORRAINE: June, why are you such a pest this morning?

JUNE: Because I think maybe it'd be better for everybody here if you'd—go along once in a while.

LORRAINE: No, I—

JUNE: Please!

LORRAINE: Even if I wanted to, who'd be here to take care of you?

JUNE: You just got done telling me I should grow up.

LORRAINE: And you just told me you didn't want to.

JUNE: Maybe I'd change my mind if I had to be on my own once in a while. Boy, I bet you haven't been on a train for—how long?

LORRAINE: Oh . . . long.

JUNE: And you like to ride trains!

LORRAINE: Yes . . .

JUNE: Mother, you used to go. All the way out to your mother's farm in Indiana.

LORRAINE: Before they castrated me.

JUNE: That's not what it was!

LORRAINE: I felt—unsexed. The heat would rise up in my throat—choke me. That happens. When you're so young and they think they have to—

JUNE: You were sick. But you're better now.

LORRAINE: I have to take care of these apples.

(JUNE *grabs her robe and dumps the apples on the ground.*)

You miserable girl! Pick up those apples! Go on! Pick them up!

(JUNE *does so.* LORRAINE *starts to go into the house but pauses at the door.*)

Forty and forty is eighty. . . .

JUNE: Huh?

LORRAINE: (*Running a slow hand over her body as though to assure herself that it is still there.*) Most people don't live past eighty. Middle age—it comes sooner than we pretend, doesn't it?

(LORRAINE *goes into the house.* JUNE *follows, crossing to exit into the kitchen with the apples.* LORRAINE *is at the mirror, looking at herself. She slowly removes the robe and lets it fall. She pulls the nightgown close and is looking at the lines of her body as* JUNE *re-enters. Self-consciously,* LORRAINE *grabs the robe and holds it in front of herself.*) I wouldn't have anything to wear.

JUNE: Boy, you really should buy clothes once in a while.

LORRAINE: I do.

JUNE: I mean, new ones. Not from the Outgrown Shoppe.

LORRAINE: Your father started his sheet metal business in that garage back there—with a secondhand brake and a secondhand welding machine. But that man was a doorbanger, believe you me! Now he's got a shop out where the old dairy used to be—but he's still using secondhand machines. Secondhand didn't stop him.

JUNE: Secondhand clothes are different! They have a funny smell and—everybody knows.

LORRAINE: Pride goes before a fall.

JUNE: Okay, forget it.

LORRAINE: I did see a pretty fall dress in Dives' Basement for $3.44 when I was buying the bathroom curtains yesterday. . . .

(JUNE *turns with surprise and they look at each other for a moment before* LORRAINE *turns away again.*)

But the stores wouldn't even be open before traintime.

JUNE: You've got to have something—yeah! That green dress! The one Danielle's mother sent to the rummage sale in the synagogue basement.

LORRAINE: Oh, I don't know—those wives of the Veterans of Foreign Wars dress to kill.

JUNE: But if we brush your gray coat real good and—maybe make up a corsage of the yellow mums—they're still nice—!

LORRAINE: I'm afraid—he might feel ashamed of me. I think he does sometimes. . . .

JUNE: (*Surprised.*) You do want to go, don't you?

LORRAINE: Oh, I—don't know—June—I—

JUNE: You do!

LORRAINE: Maybe it would help—maybe I wouldn't feel so—if I got out of the house sometimes—

JUNE: Yes!

LORRAINE: But he might not—

JUNE: Oh he'll be glad if you go along.

LORRAINE: I don't know—

JUNE: Get dressed! I'll brush your coat for you.

LORRAINE: No—I can't leave a girl your age alone in the house.

JUNE: I'll get Danielle to come over and spend the night!

LORRAINE: (*As* JUNE *gently pushes her to the stairs.*) Oh—this is crazy—

JUNE: Mother, do it. Okay? I dare you! Hey, double dare!

(LORRAINE *goes upstairs.* JUNE *watches her go, then takes a deep breath and hurries to the phone where she looks up a number in the directory and hastily dials. Entering outside is* DANIELLE, *dressed for the day in her saddle shoes, sox, skirt, and sweater, perhaps with a cheerleading letter on it. There are ribbons in her shoulder-length hair.* JUNE *speaks into the phone.*)

Yes. Hello . . . Would you please look around and tell me if Mr. Wallace Eisenhart is there? . . . You ought to know him—he eats there just about every morning . . . Well, he's about forty-two and has dark hair and is wearing a gray suit . . . I think he's with a woman named Margey . . . Could I speak to him please? I'm his daughter and it's kind of an emergency.

(DANIELLE *familiarly enters the house without knocking.*)

DANIELLE: Heeeeey, June!

JUNE: Yeah, hey. I'm on the phone.

DANIELLE: (*Happily.*) Hey, what a day! Yesterday after school I even cleaned all the junk out of my desk. Here I stand before you—purged of my 1942 menstrual calendar!

JUNE: You look really neat, Dannie. Where'd you get the new shoes?

DANIELLE: Dives. Non-rationed. Saved my shoe stamp.

JUNE: (*Into phone.*) Hello, Dad? . . . Yeah, I know but I—wanted to tell you right away . . . Nothing's exactly wrong but—Well, Mother's decided to go along with you on your trip to the dedication of that soldiers' thing this weekend . . . I said—(*Very fast.*)—you'd better come home and talk to her because she's upstairs getting dressed to go!

(*Quickly JUNE hangs up. The phone rings almost immediately. She picks it up, breaking the connection, then gently replaces the receiver.*)

DANIELLE: Your mother is—?

JUNE: Yeah.

DANIELLE: What happened to her?

JUNE: I talked her into it.

DANIELLE: But, June—your Mom and Dad aren't—

JUNE: Hey, the cards tole me it was going to be okay!

DANIELLE: The cards are okay for impressing boys and telling who's going to take you to the Football Hop but this isn't playing.

JUNE: I don't *play* with cards! I believe in them.

DANIELLE: Oh, boy.

JUNE: I believe in Isis and the moon. I'm a pagan.

DANIELLE: You know what I believe? I believe your old man is going to blitz you for this.

JUNE: I don't care! It'll keep him from going up there with—Margey.

DANIELLE: Margey Bergman.

JUNE: Bergman—? How do you know?

DANIELLE: Oh. I saw them.

JUNE: When?

DANIELLE: Saturday a week. Coming out of some bar.

JUNE: Why didn't you tell me?

DANIELLE: I figured you got enough trouble around here.

JUNE: Do you know who she is?

DANIELLE: Yeah. Some blond typist my brother Morey used to date.

JUNE: Is she pretty?

DANIELLE: Well, she looks a little like Ann Sheridan. Only not quite so—(DANIELLE *indicates big breasts.*)

JUNE: Poor mother . . . (*She gets a worn coat from a closet, hunts about for a clothes brush, and vigorously brushes the coat.*) Well, it doesn't matter what Margey Bergman looks like. Mother'll be the one riding away to the mountains with him. *She'll* be the one in the hotel room with him tonight.

DANIELLE: June, you are nuts.

JUNE: Go get some yellow mums for a corsage!

(DANIELLE *goes out of the house, leaving the door open so she can talk; she picks yellow mums which are beside the porch in a sheltered spot. She re-enters the house when she has a few nice flowers.*)

Hurry up, Mother! Dad'll be home soon.

LORRAINE: (*Off.*) I got only one other speed and that's slower than this one.

DANIELLE: You know what? All those dopey romance stories she used to read out loud to you went to your head.

JUNE: We read more than romances out loud.

DANIELLE: Yeah, you told me. The whole story of the Bible.

JUNE: I liked it. It was gruesome.

DANIELLE: So are you.

JUNE: Know something, Dannie?—I always used to love school—studying—reading. It made all this other stuff here at home sort of okay. You know? But lately I feel so restless.

All the time. I don't even get a kick out of typing class any more. I mean, this whole town is changing, Danielle! Even your mother's talking about getting a job in the parachute factory. A lot of the kids are being drafted right out of high school! And here we sit, doing homework and going to the movies.

DANIELLE: That's very interesting but the trouble is I just don't believe your Mom's going to let her little Junebaby sit alone for a whole weekend.

JUNE: Don't call me that!

DANIELLE: I didn't mean anything.

JUNE: I told her you could stay with me.

DANIELLE: June . . .

JUNE: Can you?

DANIELLE: Can I! (*Joyfully hugging her.*) Yes!

JUNE: —what—?

DANIELLE: June, listen—No, maybe you shouldn't listen. Just remember—whatever happens. I'm doing you a favor. (*At phone.*) Hello, Operator! I want to place a collect call to Philadelphia . . . Come on, Operator—how can all the circuits be busy this early? . . . It is important . . . 54-1515 . . . From Danielle Silverman. I'll hang on.

JUNE: What're you doing?

DANIELLE: Arguing with the Operator. Now she wants me to limit my call to five minutes. I'm telling you—you'd think this was the telephone company's own personal war.

JUNE: But I mean, who're you calling?

DANIELLE: (*Hand over mouthpiece.*) I came over early to ask you to give me an alibi for tonight.

JUNE: Oh, Dannie, I hate to do that. When Mrs. Silverman looks at me and asks where we went, I never know what to say.

DANIELLE: Yeah, but you're a good actress so it never shows . . .

JUNE: Am I?

DANIELLE: (*Into phone.*) Hi. This is Martin's cousin. Is he there? . . . Will you hurry and get him?—I think I've only got four minutes left. (*Hand over mouthpiece again.*) Anyway, this time you won't have to lie. I can stay here tonight and that solves all our problems—yours and mine.

JUNE: Huh?

DANIELLE: (*Into phone.*) Marty! This is Danielle! . . . Yeah, hello! . . . Look, plans have changed a little . . . No, we don't have to go there. You and your buddy can come here. It's 1416 Highland Avenue . . . My girlfriend's parents are going away for the weekend so we have the whole house to ourselves!

JUNE: (*Aghast.*) Dannie!

DANIELLE: (*Still into phone.*) Yeah, swell . . . Well, you get her. I get Tony . . . You met her—June Eisenhart.

JUNE: (*Pulling at her.*) Cut it out, Dannie!

DANIELLE: She's as old as I am. (*Trying to shake off* JUNE.) Knock it off, June!

JUNE: They can't come here!

DANIELLE: (*Quickly; into phone.*) Got to go now, Marty! See you guys around eight-thirty! (DANIELLE *hangs up, preventing* JUNE *from grabbing phone.*)

JUNE: Call right back and tell them not to come!

DANIELLE: The phone company wouldn't like that.

JUNE: Then I'll do it—

(DANIELLE *picks up the phone to guard it.*)

You have some nerve. Inviting strangers here without asking!

DANIELLE: My cousin Marty is no stranger.

JUNE: I don't know him that good. Even if I did—

DANIELLE: For crying out loud, this is their last furlough before they go overseas! Marty can't go all the way home to Seattle—there isn't time. I mean, he doesn't have wings —he can't fly. So he's staying with his buddy's family for part of his leave and with my Mom for the rest. He's due here tomorrow.

JUNE: Then why is he coming up tonight—No, don't tell me!

DANIELLE: June. Remember that dream you told me about last week?

JUNE: No.

DANIELLE: You lie.

JUNE: I shouldn't have told you.

DANIELLE: You know what it means when you dream you're not a virgin any more? That you've done it with a guy?

JUNE: Dannie—

DANIELLE: It means—you—are—ready.

JUNE: I am not ready! You think this is something like giving out assignments in school? ''You are now ready to take this civics test.'' And you even get the room number and the time. It can't be like that. Not for me. All—set up. Having soldiers coming here expecting it. In my own house. I'm not going to do it like that!

DANIELLE: Nobody said you had to do it.

JUNE: It's what they're expecting, isn't it?

DANIELLE: Fellows are always expecting. So they get used to disappointments.

JUNE: I wish boys were like they are in the stories I get from the library at school. Nice. Instead of always thinking about—that.

DANIELLE: How do you know what boys think about? You never go out with them.

JUNE: Neither do you.

DANIELLE: Huh?

JUNE: You don't go out with *boys*. Just soldiers. Your mother worries about that, you know.

DANIELLE: June, those soldiers need me.

JUNE: I think that's terrible! To be needed just for—that.

DANIELLE: Sometimes *I* think there's something wrong with you.

JUNE: There's nothing wrong with being a virgin. My mother was a virgin when she got married.

DANIELLE: I bet that's the only reason your old man married her.

JUNE: He loved her! Then.

DANIELLE: June, you know how I hate to lie to my Mom. Most of the time she's even waiting up for me. I'll never forget my first time . . . You remember I told you about that guy in the Signal Corps named Whitey?—Well, afterward—coming in—

JUNE: Stop it, Dannie!

DANIELLE: Okay, but what I'm trying to tell you is that it wouldn't have to be that way for you! Sneaking into your house alone after your first time. You'd have a whole night —a whole weekend. You could take all the time you wanted. I could, too, for a change. See, Marty's got this buddy—Tony. He says I'll go gaga over him. And I was supposed to dig up a girl for Marty.

JUNE: But you were going to get one of those Defense girls you go to the bars with, not me.

DANIELLE: Only because you never want to go along with the gang. Come on, Juney. You like Martin. I know you like Martin. I might like Martin myself if he wasn't like a brother to me.

JUNE: But, Dannie, for me it's just not going to be—like this.

DANIELLE: How's it going to be?

JUNE: Well, there'll be this really colossal guy—who looks like David Niven—only with eyes more like a poet's. And we're going to be together for days . . . just talking and playing music and reciting poetry. And then . . . one day. . . .

DANIELLE: Yeah?

JUNE: In spring. Under trees with blossom petals falling down—it'll happen. Just sort of—accidentally.

DANIELLE: Marty's going to be someplace on a second front when your dumb apple trees bloom again. Where's your patriotism?

JUNE: I'm patriotic!

DANIELLE: Then think about the soldiers.

JUNE: I do! It's just I don't think *I* have to be the one to . . . you know.

DANIELLE: But you and me are going to be the only ones here tonight and these soldiers are being sent into battle.

JUNE: (*Turning away; after a beat.*) Dannie . . . does it hurt?

DANIELLE: What?

JUNE: The first time.

DANIELLE: Not that bad.

JUNE: I wish it was over!

DANIELLE: Do it, then it will be.

JUNE: But I'm not even sure my mother's going to go!

DANIELLE: You were a couple of minutes ago.

(*There is a screech of automobile tires outside.*)

JUNE: It's my Dad!

DANIELLE: Juney—please. About Marty and Tony—

JUNE: All right.

DANIELLE: Hot dog!

JUNE: I mean, I promise I'll think about it! I didn't say I was going to do it.

DANIELLE: But they can come?

JUNE: Yes, okay—(*Losing her nerve as she watches* WALLY *through the window as he enters and strides across the yard.*) Do you think he's going to be real mad?

DANIELLE: (*Protectively, coming to* JUNE.) So he's mad—so he'll get over it.

(WALLY *enters the house.*)

WALLY: June—

JUNE: Oh. Good morning.

WALLY: June, what the deuce was—? Danielle, do you mind getting out of here for a few minutes?

(DANIELLE *hesitates, reluctant to leave* JUNE *with her father.* JUNE *indicates that it is all right for* DANIELLE *to go.*)

DANIELLE: I'll be in the kitchen making a corsage—if anybody needs me.

(DANIELLE *exits into the kitchen with the flowers.* WALLY *does not wait until she has gone before he starts in on* JUNE.)

WALLY: What was that phone call all about?

JUNE: It was about Mother going with you this weekend.

WALLY: She's not going with me.

JUNE: Yes, she is.

WALLY: She never goes with me!

JUNE: This time she decided to.

WALLY: She knows the fellows are going to be drinking—smoking—she knows that.

JUNE: Dad, haven't you noticed how she is lately?

WALLY: No different than she's been for years.

JUNE: She's getting funny again. Like when I was a kid. Since her last operation.

WALLY: All the more reason—How'd she get this crazy idea of coming along into her head?

JUNE: I don't know.

WALLY: It's probably something you and that Jew kid friend of yours cooked up.

JUNE: Danielle didn't have anything to do with it!

WALLY: But *you* did!

JUNE: Dad, she needs to get out of this house sometimes.

WALLY: I took her to the movies last week.

JUNE: And this week you can take her on a nice trip. Boy, she'll soon be well again.

WALLY: (*Striding out into the yard as if he is leaving.*) I'd rather stay home than drag her along!

JUNE: (*Going after him.*) But she wants to go!

WALLY: Why? So she can sit there with her handkerchief over her face every time somebody lights a cigarette?

JUNE: She won't do that again.

WALLY: I ought to wallop you for this, big as you are.

JUNE: Why can't you be nice to her—for just one weekend?

WALLY: Because she spoils everything for me. Like you. You're growing up to be just like her, you know that?

JUNE: I am not!

WALLY: Look at you. Some pair for a man like me to have for a family.

JUNE: I'm sorry.

WALLY: So am I! I'm sorry it was the boy that died.

(JUNE *recoils and runs into the house to sit at her piano in silent misery.*)

Wait a minute—I didn't mean that the way it sounded—Oh, shit.

(WALLY *hesitates, disturbed. He goes into the house again.*)

WALLY: All I mean is, I wish he'd lived. We'd have been more of a—family. . . . Well, a man can't take a girl like you to ball games—fishing—places I like to go. Hang a blue star in the window because your son's in the service and you're damn proud of him. Things like that. That's all I meant.

JUNE: I'm sorry.

WALLY: Quit saying that! Don't be sorry. Be something else. No damn wonder I hate to hang around this house.

JUNE: It wasn't my idea.

WALLY: What?

JUNE: About Mother. She really wants to go.

WALLY: She never wanted to go before. What's so special about this weekend? Except it's Armistice Day?

JUNE: It's the Feast of Samhain.

WALLY: The what?

JUNE: That was an old festival they used to celebrate. Early in November. The Druids. It was the beginning of winter and kind of a time apart from the rest of the year. The dead were supposed to be able to—

WALLY: I don't want to hear that heathen talk! Your mother is a Christian woman. Whatever else she is, she is a Christian woman. My God. You're not going to sit there and tell me she wants to go along so she can celebrate some pagan holiday? My God.

JUNE: I didn't mean—

WALLY: I'm going to get her to talk to her minister about you. You keep this up, young lady, and we're going to have to reserve a room at the rest farm for you like we had for her that time. You mark my words.

JUNE: What're you getting so mad about? I only—

(LORRAINE *appears on the stairs. She has dressed up. Unfortunately, her dress is ten years out of style, circa mid-1930s. However, her outfit should not be a caricature; just sadly out of date. She carries a cheap suitcase and clutches a square old purse. Tentatively she smiles at* WALLY, *then frowns to cover her confusion and perhaps seek an escape.*)

LORRAINE: I wonder if I flushed the toilet.

JUNE: Never mind, Mother. I'll get it later.

LORRAINE: (*Slowly coming down.*) Wally . . . ?

WALLY: Yeah.

LORRAINE: I thought I'd—

WALLY: June told me that you—

LORRAINE: I haven't been on a train in years. I used to like trains, remember? And—

WALLY: Lorraine, I don't even know if we can get seats. We might have to stand all the way.

LORRAINE: Oh, I don't mind.

WALLY: But it's pretty far up to the center of the state—

LORRAINE: Don't you want me to come with you, Wally?

WALLY: Oh, sure! Of course I do. I just thought—you know how the fellows are.

LORRAINE: I'll try not to mind. I'll try.

WALLY: Like you tried the last time my brother was here? Sitting around with a big handky over your face? Crap. A man can't even light a cigarette in this house without you—

LORRAINE: I wouldn't do that again! Really, I wouldn't.

JUNE: She only did it that one time. She didn't know everybody'd get mad about it.

WALLY: You keep out of this!

LORRAINE: Don't you start picking on June.

WALLY: Don't you start jumping down my throat every time I talk to the kid.

LORRAINE: Let her be, Wally! It's not her fault you married me.

WALLY: . . . Yeah, sure. Sure. (*With pseudo enthusiasm.*) Okay. Well. This is—just fine!

JUNE: Dannie! You got the corsage ready?

DANIELLE: (*Off.*) Is it safe to come out? (DANIELLE *enters from the kitchen. She has a homemade corsage of yellow mums tied with a faded ribbon.*) 'Morning, Mrs. Eisenhart!

JUNE: (*Of the corsage.*) Hey, that's keen.

LORRAINE: I'm going away with Wally this weekend, Danielle. Can you stay here with Juney?

DANIELLE: (*Pinning the corsage on* LORRAINE.) Oh, sure. Glad to.

LORRAINE: Take good care of her. You know where the games are. On the shelf in the—

JUNE: (*Helping her put on her coat.*) We'll be okay. You just have a good time.

LORRAINE: Oh, I don't know—maybe I shouldn't—

JUNE: (*Hastily.*) And don't worry about me!

LORRAINE: If you use any cans, don't forget to flatten them and put them in the war effort basket.

JUNE: Sure.

LORRAINE: And keep the doors locked at all times, girls.

DANIELLE: That's what my mother always tells me.

LORRAINE: She's a sensible woman. There are lots of strange soldiers around town.

WALLY: (*Impatiently.*) Well, come on, if you're coming. There are some calls I must make from the station.

LORRAINE: (*Looking at their phone.*) Couldn't you—?

WALLY: Businessmen don't get up this early. I'd better do it at the last minute—from a phone booth.

(*Unhappily,* WALLY *exits.* LORRAINE *kisses* JUNE, *waves to* DANIELLE, *then follows* WALLY.)

JUNE: (*Calling after them.*) Hey, this is like your second honeymoon, isn't it? I bet you'll have a swell time!

(LORRAINE *exits, waving. There is the sound of a car starting up, then pulling away with an angry grinding of gears.*)

DANIELLE: (*Gleefully hugging* JUNE.) We made it!

JUNE: Funny . . . how the house suddenly got so quiet.

DANIELLE: You haven't ever been alone here, have you?

(JUNE *shakes her head.*)

I'll go home and tell my mother and get my stuff.

JUNE: Okay.

DANIELLE: (*Pausing.*) June? Will you be okay?

JUNE: Sure.

DANIELLE: It's going to be a big weekend, Juney! For everybody!

JUNE: Yeah . . .

(JUNE *has gone into the yard and to the tree.* DANIELLE *follows her.*)

DANIELLE: Sometimes you give me the creeps. I don't know why . . . sometimes this place gives me the creeps. . . .

JUNE: (*Staring up into the tree.*) No blossoms, Dannie. Just windfall apples.

[END OF ACT ONE]

ACT TWO

It is evening of the same day. A chilling November darkness has settled, one which hints of the coming winter which will finally wither the last flowers of the year. The lamps in the house are lit, but outside are blue shadows and the lingering, cidery odor of old apples. Beyond the fence, weak rays from an inadequate street light fall, slanted and yellowish. Two soldiers, TONY *and* MARTIN, *enter the yard with* MARTIN *in the lead. Both are neat in appearance in their World War II PFC uniforms.* MARTIN *is tall and slender, with gentle eyes.* TONY *is more stocky and coarse. He carries quart bottles of beer in a paper bag. Their attitude is uncertain, even shy, as they stop and look around.*

TONY: Think this is it?

MARTIN: Must be.

TONY: See a path or—?

MARTIN: Hard to see anything—

TONY: (*Moving forward.*) Spooky dump, isn't it? (*Stopping.*) Oh, shit!

MARTIN: What's wrong?

TONY: I stepped in something—

MARTIN: (*Coming to look.*) It's just an apple, Tony.

TONY: Yeah, but now I got apple guts all over my shoe!

MARTIN: Wipe it on the grass.

TONY: You don't walk into no dame's house with dirty shoes.

MARTIN: Says who?

TONY: Says me. My old lady near knocked off my block one time for that. And my sisters—! And—all dames. Lend me your handky.

MARTIN: That far I won't go, even for a buddy.

TONY: (*Getting out his own handky and cleaning his shoe.*) Mama Mia . . . What's that funny smell? Smells almost like the wine my Uncle Mario used to make.

MARTIN: Must be the apples.

TONY: What is this—a farm?

MARTIN: Was. I guess. A long time ago. Come on, dogface. Your shoes are clean enough.

TONY: I don't want to make her mad.

MARTIN: They'll think we're not coming.

TONY: I hope this dame is worth the trip.

MARTIN: We were coming up anyhow.

TONY: But tomorrow. I bet I'd have made it with Alice tonight.

MARTIN: You didn't make it with her the seven days we were in Philly.

TONY: But I was going to try a new line.

MARTIN: Yeah?

TONY: "Alice honey, I'm going overseas and I might be killed. Maybe this is the last time for me—" I hear it gets them every time. You ought to try it, Marty.

MARTIN: No.

TONY: What's the matter with you?

MARTIN: Nothing!

TONY: You think you don't need a line? Marty, a Clark Gable you are not. Well, maybe I'm not either—but *I* bring presents.

MARTIN: Beer isn't a present. Come on.

TONY: Ring the doorbell, buddy, and tell her not to take off her bra—I don't have time to chew the fat.

MARTIN: Knock it off, Tony!

TONY: Hey, is it bugging you I'm going to lay your cousin?

MARTIN: No!

TONY: Sure you ain't got hot nuts for her yourself?

MARTIN: She's like a sister to me! She lived with my family in Seattle.

TONY: Yeah, well, you've been acting funny ever since we left Philly.

MARTIN: It's just—I don't want you to get the wrong idea about her.

TONY: The only idea I got is that I'm going to screw her.

MARTIN: Dammit, Tony!

TONY: Isn't that what we came for?

MARTIN: Dannie's not like Alice.

TONY: You mean she don't have to get drunk to do it?

MARTIN: Dannie's the kind of girl you bring flowers to, not beer.

TONY: (*Shrugging, then grabbing some of the flowers growing beside the porch.*) They going to make breakfast for us tomorrow?

MARTIN: Boy, you want everthing, don't you?

TONY: Yeah. Everything.

(MARTIN *rings the doorbell. Inside,* JUNE *and* DANIELLE *have already come down the stairs. They have dressed up, now wearing party dresses with wide net skirts, flowers in their hair, high heels, stockings with seams, flashy jewelry, dark red lipstick, pageboy hairdos, all circa World War II.* JUNE *no longer looks so much like an ugly duckling. Obviously someone—*DANIELLE*—has put in time helping her fix her hair and makeup, and has lent her an adequate dress.*)

DANIELLE: They're here!

JUNE: Wait a minute—!

DANIELLE: We can't let them stand out there—

JUNE: How do I look?

DANIELLE: Like—Bette Davis.

JUNE: I do?

DANIELLE: So just try to act like Bette Davis tonight, will you? Natural but—sophisticated. Like she would if Paul Henreid was coming.

JUNE: I'll try.

(*The doorbell rings again.* DANIELLE *opens the door.*)

DANIELLE: Welcome home!

MARTIN: (*As they embrace affectionately, genuinely glad to see each other. For a few seconds the others are forgotten.*) Dannie!

DANIELLE: Martin! You look really keen! Marty—I never saw you like this—that uniform! It's beautiful! Oh—How long's it been?

MARTIN: Too damn long!

DANIELLE: I'm so glad to see you!

MARTIN: (*Swinging her around.*) Hey—you're something yourself. Tony! Isn't she a beaut? Tony! Dannie!

TONY: Do I get a hug too?

DANIELLE: (*Embracing him lightly.*) Welcome, Tony!

MARTIN: Well—June! Hello.

JUNE: Yes. Hello.

DANIELLE: Tony, this is my best friend, June.

TONY: Hi, June. Say, I like those old apple trees you got here. They sure are big and round, yes sir.

JUNE: Apple trees are always round. Like apples. Pear trees are oblong like pears.

TONY: Yeah? That's very interesting. (*Turning to* DANIELLE.) Brought you some flowers.

DANIELLE: (*Taking the mums without enthusiasm.*) Thanks.

TONY: And beer.

DANIELLE: (*Happily.*) Thanks!

TONY: (*Aside to* MARTIN.) And you said they don't like beer. She's okay, Marty, okay.

MARTIN: June, you were just a kid last time I was here to visit Aunt Rose.

TONY: Well, she don't look like no kid tonight.

DANIELLE: It's the war. Everybody's growing up fast.

TONY: Got to. Never know how long it's going to last.

DANIELLE: Us or the war?

TONY: Both. They say Hitler's got a secret weapon.

MARTIN: So does Uncle Sam. Here's Tony—the Army's secret weapon.

TONY: That's me!

DANIELLE: Let's have some beer! June, will you get glasses?

JUNE: Oh. Sure. Uh—maybe somebody'd like 7-Up?

TONY: 7-Up?

(DANIELLE *pokes* JUNE.)

MARTIN: Don't you drink beer?

JUNE: No. I never have. (JUNE *goes into the kitchen.* TONY *opens a bottle of beer with an opener he carries for emergencies and drinks out of the bottle.*)

MARTIN: She's never even had a glass of beer?

DANIELLE: But aside from that, what'd you think?

MARTIN: I don't know.

DANIELLE: With June, that means we're doing okay.

TONY: How old is she?

DANIELLE: Same as me.

MARTIN: Sixteen.

TONY: She don't seem that old.

DANIELLE: Her mother doesn't let her out much.

TONY: Speaking of the kid's mother—

DANIELLE: Won't be back until tomorrow night.

TONY: (*Pushing aside some books, flopping down on the sofa with his feet on a coffee table.*) This sure beats Camp Dix!

DANIELLE: The only thing we've got to remember is to keep the door locked.

TONY: Huh?

MARTIN: Why?

DANIELLE: June's mother is afraid to have us girls alone here with all the strange soldiers in town.

MARTIN: She's right. There are a lot of strange soldiers around. Look at Tony here.

(TONY *lifts his beer in a toast to that remark.* JUNE *enters with glasses and an opener and a quart of 7-Up.* TONY *rises and pours a glass of beer for* DANIELLE.)

DANIELLE: AND if we run out of beer . . . (*She gets a bottle of wine from a bag she has brought with her.*)

JUNE: Dannie—where'd you get that?

DANIELLE: My mother always keeps a couple of bottles around for Friday nights.

JUNE: But—that's holy wine! We shouldn't—

DANIELLE: What's it to you? Evangelists don't even have holy wine.

JUNE: Evangelicals.

TONY: What's a Evangelical?

DANIELLE: Somebody who drinks Welch's grape juice at Communion.

TONY: I didn't know anybody did that.

DANIELLE: Tony, I think this beer's getting warm.

TONY: Where's the refrigerator?

JUNE: It's an icebox. I'll show you.

DANIELLE: (*Intercepting her.*) Tony can find it.

TONY: I'll take a cold shower and be right back.

(TONY *exits into the kitchen with his bottles of beer.* DANIELLE *turns her back to* MARTIN *and mouths "Bette Davis" at* JUNE. JUNE *straightens and moves to* MARTIN *with a smile pasted onto her face.*)

JUNE: Would you like a beer?

MARTIN: I'll take 7-Up.

(*This surprises* JUNE, *who looks back over her shoulder at* DANIELLE, *who impatiently motions her toward the 7-Up.* JUNE *goes to pour two glasses of soft drink.*)

JUNE: Maybe after we have a drink, we could all go to a movie. Betty Grable and Judy Garland are in Pigskin Parade.

DANIELLE: (*Posing.*) What's Grable got that I haven't got?

MARTIN: Her picture all over our barracks.

JUNE: Do they put up any pictures of Bette Davis?

MARTIN: I haven't seen any.

JUNE: Oh.

(MARTIN *gets a flask of whiskey out of his pocket and pours shots into the 7-Up.*)

DANIELLE: Well, well, well!

MARTIN: I got class, cousin. Tony's the one who shows up with beer.

(TONY *reenters, singing "The Beer Barrel Polka."*)

JUNE: (*As* MARTIN *hand her a glass.*) I don't—

DANIELLE: (*Quickly.*) What you mean, Juney, is that you NEVER. It doesn't mean you DON'T. Just sip it. It won't hurt you to sip it.

(JUNE, *holding the glass, recalls scenes of cocktail parties in many, many films. The feel of the glass in her hand gives her a sense of sophistication. Of being one with the platinum blondes of Hollywood. She experiments with holding it.*)

MARTIN: Let's drink a toast! (*Lifting glass.*) To Armistice Day!

DANIELLE: That's the dumbest toast I ever heard.

TONY: I'll drink to anything. (*Lifting his glass.*) Here's to Armistice Day!

(*They drink, naturally, except for* JUNE, *who takes a sip, now interested to know what it tastes like. She doesn't like it.*)

Know what my Mom says? She says they just waited to start again until they had more cannon fodder. That's me. Cannon Fodder. But my friends call me Cannon.

MARTIN: Come on, Tony. You're having the time of your life.

TONY: But don't forget I ain't been overseas yet. I don't know if I'm going to think it's so great once they start shooting at me.

DANIELLE: Chicken.

TONY: Look who's talking here. You're a skirt, honey, nobody shoots at skirts.

JUNE: (*Brightly.*) If you don't like Betty Grable or Judy Garland, how about Errol Flynn?

TONY: Huh?

DANIELLE: (*Casually elaborate as she gets out a pack of cigarettes and offers them around.*) June goes to the movies. A lot.

JUNE: Next summer I'm going to get a job as an usherette. (JUNE *accepts a cigarette, has difficulties but finally manages a small puff imitation of Bette Davis.*) Danielle, did you know that the Happy Boys orchestra is playing down at the Elks Club tonight?

DANIELLE: June. (*This is a warning not to overdo it.*) I brought my Glen Miller records along.

TONY: Swell. I want to stay home tonight.

MARTIN: How do you like your drink?

TONY: Great beer! How did I know to bring my own brand?

MARTIN: Not you, stupid. Her.

JUNE: (*Who has been taken down a peg and, losing Bette Davis, is adrift in her own personality.*) I . . . Well . . . I think that stuff sort of spoils the taste of the 7-Up.

MARTIN: Yeah? (*Takes a shot straight out of his flask.*) Nope. It's the 7-Up spoils the taste of the other stuff. Try it this way.

JUNE: No!

MARTIN: I'm only kidding, June.

TONY: Who plays the piano around here?

JUNE: Me.

DANIELLE: She's good, too. Plays for everything at school.

TONY: Know "The Beer Barrel Polka"?

JUNE: No.

TONY: How come? I thought everybody knew "The Beer Barrel Polka."

MARTIN: Tony thinks they're going to make it the national anthem any day now.

JUNE: I wanted to get the sheet music for it but my mother wouldn't let me.

DANIELLE: Her old lady's some kind of nut. I mean, about drinking.

JUNE: She never forgave President Roosevelt for repealing Prohibition.

MARTIN: Play something, June. Anything.

JUNE: (*This is firm ground on which she can stand.*) Okay. (*She sits at the piano and her fingers wander into something gently classical.* TONY *and* DANIELLE *have been poised to dance.*)

DANIELLE: June—we can't dance to that!

JUNE: Sorry.

MARTIN: I think we should put on some of Dannie's records so we can all dance.

DANIELLE: Good idea!

(DANIELLE *and* TONY *select a record and wind up the victrola.*)

JUNE: I don't jitterbug.

MARTIN: Why not?

JUNE: I've got two left feet.

MARTIN: That's my specialty. People with two left feet.

JUNE: You're no teacher.

MARTIN: You're hurting my feelings.

JUNE: Boys don't get hurt feelings.

(DANIELLE *and* TONY *are dancing.*)

MARTIN: Who told you that?

JUNE: (*Realizing she has come too close to expressing her own feelings and neglecting party talk; she covers by taking a big swallow of her drink.*) This really isn't all that bad.

MARTIN: None of it is, June. (*He pulls her to her feet and they move into a dance;* JUNE *is very awkward.*) Let yourself go.

JUNE: I can't—

MARTIN: Sure, you can. Just do what I do.

(*Despite her protests, he manages to get her into some semblance of a stiff-legged jitterbug. She does not, however, relax into it and move effortlessly. The music ends abruptly.*)

DANIELLE: That was fun.

TONY: Let's put on another record.

(DANIELLE *and* TONY *hunt another record and start the victrola again.*)

JUNE: Tell me about Seattle.

MARTIN: Seattle? . . . Lots of steps.

JUNE: Steps?

MARTIN: On the hills. It's built on hills. Water all around. The Sound.

JUNE: Do you have a girlfriend there?

MARTIN: No.

(*A slow, romantic Miller record is now playing.* TONY *turns out one of the lights.* TONY *and* DANNIE *drift into each other's arms effortlessly, as if they belong together.* MARTIN *watches them, then resolutely turns toward* JUNE. *There is a strained moment, then* JUNE *sits.*)

MARTIN: Drink up.

JUNE: I don't—

MARTIN: (*Glancing at* DANIELLE *and* TONY *again.*) You've got to learn to do something. If you don't dance, at least you can drink.

(JUNE *accepts the wisdom of this reasoning and dutifully glugs down more of her drink since that is easier than dancing. Throughout this act, drinking continues. Each character progresses to drunkenness at his or her own rate but all are affected by the alcohol they consume throughout.*)

How'd you and Dannie get to be such good friends?

JUNE: I don't know—her mother likes me.

MARTIN: Then how come you're not her mother's friend?

JUNE: Well, I am. I guess. But I go to school with Dannie.

MARTIN: That gives you a lot in common.

JUNE: There's a lot to talk about if you go to the same school. She's been good to me. Dannie. At school. Kids can be pretty mean sometimes if you're. . . . We do things for each other, Dannie and me. She can get out more if her mother thinks she's with me.

MARTIN: Good old innocent Aunt Rose.

JUNE: You really like her, don't you?

MARTIN: She's almost more like my mother than my own mother.

JUNE: I thought it was something like that. I mean, to spend you last furlough here instead of going home.

MARTIN: (*That "last furlough" stabbed him; he is constantly aware of* DANIELLE *and* TONY *together.*) My parents aren't like Aunt Rose and Uncle Gene. They're Orthodox, you know.

JUNE: No, I didn't—

MARTIN: That means they're . . . Anyhow, I didn't want to go back there. What's the good of fighting about things like that now?

JUNE: Oh. Yeah. I know what you mean. My parents—

MARTIN: So I figured I'd go along home with my buddy Tony—

(DANIELLE *and* TONY *have stopped dancing and sit on the sofa to neck.* MARTIN *reacts to this with another stiff drink.*)

JUNE: I'll have another one, too.

MARTIN: Think you can handle it?

JUNE: (*A Joan Crawford.*) Of course.

MARTIN: This may just turn out to be your social grace, June. (*Pours drink for her.*) Got any food around here? We didn't eat much at the station.

DANIELLE: (TONY *has been getting heavy.*) Cut it out, Tony.

MARTIN: Hey, Danielle! How about some eats?

DANIELLE: (*Shoving* TONY *away.*) Yeah. Swell.

TONY: I took you for a good sport, Dannie.

DANIELLE: It takes me more than ten minutes with a new guy to be a good sport, sport.

TONY: Okay. I can spare fifteen.

DANIELLE: What's your Mom got in the icebox, June?

TONY: Besides beer.

JUNE: (*The Hostess.*) I'll see what I have in my icebox. (JUNE *exits into the kitchen.*)

DANIELLE: (*Watching* MARTIN *take another shot.*) Aren't you hitting that juice pretty heavy, Marty?

MARTIN: (*Putting the blame the only place he dare.*) Dannie, why didn't you warn me?

DANIELLE: She'll grow on you.

MARTIN: This leave isn't that long she should grow on me.

DANIELLE: Give her a chance.

MARTIN: Why is she so . . . ?

DANIELLE: Her mother's a little nuts and her father's not home a lot.

MARTIN: So what does that make her?

DANIELLE: A virgin.

TONY: Why didn't somebody tell me? Hey, buddy, want to trade.

MARTIN: Danielle is my cousin!

TONY: So what? I've been screwing my cousin Edith for years.

DANIELLE: But Marty here is too Orthodox to do that, aren't you, Martin?

MARTIN: I'm not Orthodox! I'm hardly even Jewish any more.

DANIELLE: (*Laughing.*) Oh, sure! Marty, don't forget how long I lived in your house—

MARTIN: I even eat bacon now! Don't I, Tony?

DANIELLE: *You*—?

MARTIN: Me!

DANIELLE: I bet you don't go to services—

MARTIN: You know where I ought to go? Over to Aunt Rose's tonight.

TONY: Hey, buddy—

DANIELLE: (*Intercepting* MARTIN, *who has started toward the door.*) Marty! Forget all that stuff. Your folks—mine. They're not here tonight. June's here.

MARTIN: June.

DANIELLE: You don't realize the problems this girl has got. You should hear the stuff she tells me.

TONY: About what?

DANIELLE: Spooky stuff. About ghosts. Sometimes she knows when things are going to happen before they happen.

TONY: So do I. I know what's going to happen here tonight. Give me my crystal ball! Eeney-meeney—I see a bedroom . . .

MARTIN: Shut up, Tony.

TONY: Damn it, Marty—I want to have fun! We've been inspected for overseas, buddy. This is it!

MARTIN: I know that!

TONY: You don't act it.

MARTIN: Yeah . . . I— (*He takes a drink.*) Okay! Fun. Last furlough . . . we've got to make it—fun.

DANIELLE: Marty, listen to me. June's ready.

TONY: Oh, boy.

MARTIN: What makes you think she's ready?

DANIELLE: She tells me about her dreams. You want to hear?

TONY: Yeah!

MARTIN: No.

TONY: I ask you, is this Marty, my buddy? Sounds more like my mother.

MARTIN: Okay. She's ready. So am I. (MARTIN *goes into the kitchen.*)

DANIELLE: Tony—how long's he been acting like this?

TONY: Ah, I know what's eating him. It's eating all of us guys—some more, some less. See, you get scared. When you know you're finally shipping. Not even the old man's going to be able to stop it this time.

DANIELLE: The old man?

TONY: The general. Dannie—as soon as we get back to base—we're heading overseas. Maybe—we're going to die. Marty. Me. Maybe this is our last night.

DANIELLE: Oh, Tony—

TONY: (*Moving in, pressing his advantage.*) Let's go upstairs and neck in bed.

DANIELLE: Come on—

TONY: What's wrong?

DANIELLE: I'm not that fast. I like to be coaxed.

TONY: I don't have time for coaxing.

(JUNE *and* MARTIN *enter with a tray of crackers and cheeses, pickles, and olives.*)

Well, this is not what I came for but I guess it'll have to do. Where's the mustard?

DANIELLE: I'll get it. (DANIELLE *exits into the kitchen.*)

TONY: (*Turning to* JUNE.) I was just telling Dannie, June—Marty and me—we're shipping overseas.

JUNE: I know.

TONY: Yes, sir. Overseas. A lot of guys don't make it back.

MARTIN: Shove some cheese in your mouth, Tony.

TONY: Listen, buddy. Know what I'm going to do for you? Since you don't like virgins. I'm going to break her in for you.

JUNE: I don't want you to talk like that!

MARTIN: He's only kidding, June.

TONY: (*To* JUNE.) Have an olive. Have two. Eat the whole bottle full.

JUNE: I don't like olives.

TONY: I knew it! June, that's your whole trouble. See? You got to learn to eat olives. You know the first thing my old man told me when we talked about the birds and the bees? "Anthony," he said—always called me Anthony; thought I was a saint—"Anthony, there's one thing you can count on in this world and it's about the only thing—there's a hard-on in every bottle of olives."

JUNE: Tony, stop it!

TONY: Okay. You don't like Tony the Talker—I'll give you Tony the Clown!

(DANIELLE *enters with jar of mustard.*)

DANIELLE: Here you go.

(TONY, *acting the clown, juggles his beer as he dips cheese into the mustard.*)

JUNE: Dannie—

DANIELLE: Yeah?

JUNE: I don't think this was such a good idea—Look! He's spilling beer on the floor. My mother's going to smell it and—

DANIELLE: I'll help you clean up after they go.

JUNE: And Martin's not—I don't think he likes me, Dannie.

TONY: (*Crossing his legs.*) Where's the john?

DANIELLE: Upstairs. First door on the right.

TONY: Emergency! Emergency! (TONY *bolts up the stairs.*)

JUNE: I think we ought to forget the whole thing.

DANIELLE: It's too late!

JUNE: No, it's not. You could go home. They could—Well, the Red Cross has places for them to stay.

DANIELLE: You're not ruining my big weekend, June Eisenhart! Uh uh!

MARTIN: Look, June—it'll be okay. The thing with me—I've been drinking a little too much today—that's all.

JUNE: Do you feel—a little funny?

MARTIN: You might say that. Yeah.

JUNE: So do I.

MARTIN: Eat something.

JUNE: Am I drunk?

MARTIN: No.

JUNE: I'm—something.

MARTIN: Just a little high.

JUNE: (*Giggling, then sobering.*) I don't like it.

MARTIN: June, this is why you drink.

JUNE: So I can feel like *this*?

MARTIN: (*Smiling.*) You're a funny kid.

JUNE: Judy Canova!

MARTIN: What?

JUNE: I'm not Bette Davis, I'm Judy Canova!

DANIELLE: (*Relieved.*) Everybody okay now? (*Calling up the stairs.*) Hey, Tony! Did you pass out?

(JUNE *goes to the piano and plays a few bars of an Appalachian Mountain song, singing in a nasal voice, in honor of Judy Canova.* MARTIN, *for the first time, is focusing on her and pours her another drink.* JUNE *takes a long swallow and immediately goes into an entirely different song, a moody one.* TONY *appears on the stairs with a towel over his head and holding some carnations made of toilet paper.*)

TONY: Play "Here Comes the Bride"!

(JUNE *does so.* TONY *comes down the stairs singing.*)

"Here comes a virgin—I want to lay—Let's all stop eating —and roll in the hay!"

(*They laugh.*)

Is everybody happy?

JUNE: Where'd you get the flowers?

TONY: You never saw toilet paper carnations? My sisters—they had the whole house full of toilet paper carnations. Maria—that's the youngest—she's going to be a nun —Anyway, she got so good she could whip up triple carnations out of only two sheets of toilet paper. They want to decorate the convent sometime they'll be glad they got her.

MARTIN: That's my buddy. Didn't I tell you he was great?

DANIELLE: Where'd you find him?

MARTIN: Just looked under a rock and there he was.

TONY: No, what happened—See, this one time I'm out back near the kitchen—I'm a regular on KP—the sergeant got it in for me—and there was this guy wolfing down pork chops where the other guy's couldn't see him. Like he never had a pork chop before. It gave us a lot in common. We're both nuts about pork chops.

MARTIN: Tony, you old yardbird—you're just plain nuts.

TONY: The only Jewboy in our outfit who's an undercover pork chop eater.

MARTIN: How'd you like a fist right in the teeth, dogface?

TONY: Know anybody with a fist big enough, yardbird?

(MARTIN *swings at* TONY *and they spar around, more in play than anger.*)

JUNE: Come on, you guys, cut it out!

DANIELLE: Get him, Marty!

TONY: Whose side you on?

(*This momentary distraction gives* MARTIN *a chance to grab* TONY *in a wrestling hold. They struggle, bumping into a table, knocking a vase to the floor. It breaks.*)

TONY: Hey—no fair! (TONY *goes for* MARTIN *again but* JUNE *grabs him.*)

JUNE: Stop it! You got beer all over the rug and now you broke my mother's good vase—

TONY: Those hands on me! Those virgin hands—I'm getting a hard-on.

(JUNE *releases him and jumps away.*)

MARTIN: Don't talk like a truck driver, Tony!

TONY: Nobody around here can take a joke. (*Discovering an injury of minor nature.*) Look at that! I'm hurt.

DANIELLE: Aw. A boo-boo.

TONY: It's bleeding.

DANIELLE: Hey, June—these are the brave soldiers who are going to save us from the Nazi menace.

JUNE: Well, I wish they'd go do it.

TONY: I can't unless somebody nurses me back to health.

DANIELLE: Come on. They have stuff in the medicine cabinet for that terrible wound.

TONY: Good! I'll play doctor if you'll play nurse!

(*Laughing,* DANIELLE *and* TONY *go upstairs.*)

MARTIN: Want me to glue that vase?

JUNE: She'd notice!

MARTIN: Only trying to help. Are you all right?

JUNE: I don't know . . . it's as if—my mother came back. Before—I mean, tonight—I was beginning to feel free of them—alone, you know—but when the vase broke—it's almost as if I can hear her scolding . . .

MARTIN: You're drunk.

JUNE: She almost never goes out, you know. I think her voice is in the walls of this house. You shouldn't be here. In her house.

MARTIN: We're housebroken.

JUNE: No. There's something about men—when they get together in a war—it's not like they're—well, a person-like. It's—gangs of them on Penn Street, all coming out for the war. Like they're not living in houses any more and doing things the rest of us do. Marching isn't walking.

MARTIN: You're right. It's not. But you're wrong about the voice. It's not your Mother. It's my father.

JUNE: He never lived here.

MARTIN: But in the evening—when something breaks—I hear him.

(MARTIN *goes to the stairs and looks upward, then takes a drink from his flask and goes outside. He stops on the porch, taking gulps of air, rubs a hand through his hair and then sinks to the steps to sit, dejected. In the room* JUNE *stands, surprised. She hesitates, looks up the stairs.*)

DANIELLE: (*Off; laughing.*) Take it easy! I thought you were hurt.

(JUNE *goes to the closet, gets a sweater and goes outside, softly closing the door. She sees* MARTIN, *stops, then slowly comes and sits beside him. He looks at her, then restlessly looks about at the trees.*)

MARTIN: Regular damn orchard around here.

JUNE: It's not an orchard. Just apple trees. Winter apples.

MARTIN: How come they're not autumn apples like all the other apples in my life?

JUNE: These last all winter. In cold cellars. Want one? (JUNE *gets up, finds a good apple, brings it. He doesn't take it. She places it beside him.*) They're okay to eat even when they're on the ground.

MARTIN: It's brown.

JUNE: Red-brown.

MARTIN: They're supposed to be like that?

JUNE: Uh huh. They're Russet apples.

MARTIN: Never heard of them.

JUNE: Neither did anybody else, I guess. Except—one time at Dannie's house—after her brother's bar mitzvah—at the party they had at the house—there was this old man. He asked me about these trees. He used to live here.

MARTIN: The old synagogue was near here.

JUNE: I know. Your Aunt Rose says she still misses it.

MARTIN: She doesn't believe the modern one they built in Crestview is as holy.

JUNE: Maybe it's not.

MARTIN: Nobody else seems to mind.

JUNE: But they're the ones who moved away to the new suburbs. The Silvermans stayed. And so did that old man until his children made him go. Want to hear what he told me about the apples?

MARTIN: Why not?

JUNE: Well, he said he used to dig a hole and line it with straw—put the apples in, then more straw, and finally dirt all over the top. That way, in spring, you'd have winter apples to eat even if you didn't have anything else.

MARTIN: The things they had to do to stay alive. . . .

JUNE: He said—it was like apple graves. Like they were digging apple graves. (*Pause.*) It's nice out here in the evening, isn't it?

MARTIN: (*Looking around.*) I think—maybe—I could get to like it here. Just sitting here. (*Startled by a small sound.*) What's that?

JUNE: Just another apple falling down.

MARTIN: Strange sound.

JUNE: "Blunt, rich, huddled, sound . . . "

MARTIN: A poem?

JUNE: About apples.

MARTIN: You write it?

(JUNE *shakes her head.*)

But I bet you do write poems.

JUNE: Well, sometimes. Not much happens around here to write about—I bet you're excited!

MARTIN: About what?

JUNE: Going overseas.

MARTIN: It's not a vacation. It's a war.

JUNE: It's getting away! That's what's so great about being a boy. You get away.

MARTIN: I didn't have much choice.

JUNE: But that's just it. They draft you so nobody can stop you from going.

MARTIN: What's stopping you from going?

JUNE: It's harder when you're a girl. Unless you're like Dannie. She says she's going to New York as soon as she's out of high school and I bet she will, too. We talk about that a lot. . . .

MARTIN: (*Rising and walking out under the trees.*) I think it's good the dead can't come back and see their old places—houses—orchards—

JUNE: (*Following him.*) What makes you think they can't?

MARTIN: I'm not superstitious (*Looking upward.*) It must be beautiful here in spring.

JUNE: Oh, it is.

MARTIN: I wish I could see it then. I wish . . .

(*They look at each other. They are very close.* MARTIN *gently kisses* JUNE. *There is a moment of quiet before she moves away.*)

JUNE: I think there's something I ought to tell you. Right now. I don't do—that. I'm not going to do that.

MARTIN: What?

JUNE: What you came for!

MARTIN: Oh. That.

JUNE: Didn't you?

MARTIN: I came because I wanted to talk to a girl tonight. And go to bed with a girl.

JUNE: I knew it.

MARTIN: At least I'm honest.

JUNE: That's all boys ever think about.

MARTIN: Not true.

JUNE: You can't be friends with boys. We were talking. Maybe we'd have started to talk about ghosts—I like to talk about ghosts. But all you're thinking about is—

MARTIN: I thought you wanted me to kiss you.

JUNE: Well, I didn't! . . . I guess you want to go now.

MARTIN: Uh uh.

JUNE: Don't you believe what I said?

MARTIN: Uh huh.

JUNE: Then why aren't you going?

MARTIN: A guy doesn't get to see trees full of brown apples every day, you know.

(*He sits, dejected. She shares his mood.*)

JUNE: (*Pause.*) I'm not very good company.

MARTIN: Neither am I. Maybe we're two of a kind.

JUNE: You think so?

(*He shrugs.*)

Want to talk about ghosts? I saw one.

MARTIN: Where?

JUNE: Under an old stone arch. In a cemetery. Dannie and I dared each other to go in one night. And I saw this thing— greenish white. And it just stood there—looking at me.

MARTIN: (*Lifting his flask.*) Whoo—that sounds like some of the tall tales they tell in Seattle bars.

JUNE: It's true! I saw it.

MARTIN: I believe you. That's one of my good points, June. I believe people. My mother used to have this big story she'd tell about how when she was a girl she'd taken this pilgrimage to Palestine. She even knew what the myrtle blossoms smelled like in spring on those deserts. Hadassah—you know. Now, everybody in her family—my aunts and uncles —they swear she's never been out of continental United States. But I believe her. I think she went down to the Land of Israel.

JUNE: I don't know what you mean—

MARTIN: One way or the other.

JUNE: Oh. Maybe not in her body but in her spirit?

MARTIN: Something like that.

JUNE: I thought you weren't superstitious.

MARTIN: *I'm* not. But you are so maybe you can see ghosts.

I'm not religious either but my mother is. So maybe she could go to Palestine when nobody's looking.

JUNE: I bet she did! In her spirit! I think Jewish people have a lot of spirit.

MARTIN: (*Toasting.*) Shalom.

JUNE: Want me to tell your cards?

MARTIN: Do what?

JUNE: Didn't Dannie tell you? I read cards.

MARTIN: Read—cards?

JUNE: Playing cards. Fortune telling.

MARTIN: Where'd you learn to do that?

JUNE: From my father's mother.

MARTIN: She was a gypsy fortune teller?

JUNE: She was a widow so she used to run boarding houses at the coal mines. And after work was done at night she'd make extra money reading cards for the men. She lived with us when she got old. Come on!

(JUNE *enthusiastically runs into the house.* MARTIN *shakes his head but follows her inside. She gets her cards from the piano bench.*)

MARTIN: What're they doing under all that sheet music?

JUNE: Mother doesn't like them in her house. (JUNE *does a simple layout of the cards on a table.*)

MARTIN: (*A put-on.*) We're doing all sorts of—evil—things tonight, aren't we?

JUNE: This isn't evil!

MARTIN: I don't even think it's sensible.

JUNE: (*Puzzling over cards.*) Hmmm . . . this queen . . . The Queen of Tears . . . You'd call her clubs.

MARTIN: My mother?

JUNE: Uh uh. It's a girl. See? This other card is you.

MARTIN: I didn't know I looked like *that*.

JUNE: You love her.

MARTIN: Wrong.

JUNE: Oh, I'm never wrong. I'm very good at this. Look at all those hearts—even you must be able to see there's a lot of love for somebody in this layout. (*Another card.*) But here's trouble. Something happened. (*Another card.*) Yes, here he comes. This man—black king. That's your father!

MARTIN: I don't want to hear about my father tonight. I know about my father. That's all past.

JUNE: Want to know your future?

MARTIN: No, I—

JUNE: (*Theatrically.*) Your future!

(*She turns over the last card which is the Ace of Spades.* JUNE'S *reaction, due to the drinks she has had, is slower than it would ordinarily be. She looks at the card, at him, back at the card before she can pull herself together to sweep up the cards.*)

MARTIN: (*After a beat.*) It's okay, June. I told you I wasn't superstitious.

JUNE: It wasn't THAT card!

MARTIN: I *saw* the Ace of Spades!

JUNE: But—I mean—THAT card doesn't always mean—what people think it means. Sometimes it's—trouble—war. Yes, that's it. War. You're going to war.

MARTIN: I know!

JUNE: Anyway, it's just a game. Sort of. Something to do. It gives you something to talk about when you're around people. You know? It doesn't really mean anything.

(*He takes a drink.*)

I'm sorry—

(*Pause. It is very awkward between them.* JUNE *puts away the cards, down under, burying them for tonight.* MARTIN *struggles to recover.*)

MARTIN: (*Finally.*) What do you want, June?

JUNE: Huh?

MARTIN: You want to get married?

JUNE: Oh, no.

MARTIN: Most girls do.

JUNE: Not me. I don't think I could ever relax if I was married. I can't even eat spaghetti around boys.

MARTIN: Spaghetti—?

JUNE: Well, you're really vulnerable when you eat spaghetti. I slop on myself.

(MARTIN *tries to take another slug of liquor and finds he cannot.*)

Know what I'd like to do? Go on the stage.

(*Somewhat nervously she takes the flask from his hand and puts it down.* MARTIN *permits her to do this. He leans back.*)

MARTIN: Rub my head.

JUNE: I don't know how.

MARTIN: Act like you know how.

JUNE: (*Hesitantly begins to rub his forehead and neck.*) Actually, I want to do more than act. I'd like to play music on the stage.

MARTIN: But you're so shy.

JUNE: Not when I'm on a stage.

MARTIN: I think you'd make a better writer than performer.

JUNE: Me? Oh, no.

MARTIN: Why not?

JUNE: I'm not smart enough.

MARTIN: Sure you are. And remember, I'm the first one who told you so.

JUNE: Do you feel better?

MARTIN: Yes. You acted the part very well . . . You've been acting all evening, haven't you?

JUNE: No—

MARTIN: It's okay, June.

JUNE: What'd you mean?

MARTIN: A lot of nice girls get overlooked.

JUNE: What do you know about it?

MARTIN: A lot of boys get overlooked, too.

JUNE: I don't believe you.

MARTIN: What'd I say?

JUNE: You've had girls.

MARTIN: I've been out of school for a couple of years. Twenty-one. That's getting up there. Wisdom teeth and all. So. Well. Here we are. Hey! (*Leaning in to her.*) Do your hear anything?

JUNE: No.

MARTIN: No voices?

JUNE: No.

MARTIN: We're alone. (*Earnestly.*) June. You could do a lot worse than trying it here tonight. You must be curious. I'm gentle. And I'm clean. You know me and some of my family.

JUNE: I think that's a terrible thing to say!

MARTIN: Strange. I thought I presented the case rather well.

JUNE: It's not romantic!

MARTIN: I tried romance before and it didn't work.

JUNE: When?

MARTIN: Out under the apple tree. When I kissed you.

JUNE: There's a lot to think about when you're a girl.

MARTIN: I've got rubbers in my pocket if that's what you're thinking about.

JUNE: That's awful!

MARTIN: Why? I didn't figure you'd have any. We get them free at the base.

JUNE: That isn't what you—talk about when you're trying to get a girl to—you know—make love.

MARTIN: It's what I talk about.

JUNE: No wonder you're unpopular.

MARTIN: You think that could be it? Some guys bring candy. I bring rubbers. I think it's a lot more practical. And it's a lot better for your teeth.

JUNE: You really have . . . ? In your pocket . . . ?

MARTIN: Want to see them?

JUNE: Girls don't want to see things like that!

MARTIN: Boys have to.

JUNE: I want to look at apple blossoms!

MARTIN: Apple blossoms? Well. Okay. We'll see what we can do.

(MARTIN *puts a soft record on the victrola and comes to her, close. They dance or, more accurately, move back and forth.*) Relax.

JUNE: I don't know how.

MARTIN: You smell good.

JUNE: I washed my hair.

MARTIN: In apple blossom soap.

JUNE: No, it was Breck—

MARTIN: Pretend.

JUNE: Like they do in the movies? But in the movies—Paul Henried and Bette Davis—after the camera stops they don't really . . . Do they?

MARTIN: Well, not Bette Davis.

JUNE: She just kisses them and they stop while it's still nice.

MARTIN: It's nice all the way.

JUNE: It hurts.

MARTIN: Only a little. Only at first.

JUNE: Do you really think it's nice, Marty?

MARTIN: Very nice.

JUNE: I saw pictures once. Dannie's brother had—

MARTIN: (*Gently pulling her onto the sofa.*) Dannie's right.

JUNE: About what?

MARTIN: She says you're ready.

JUNE: She told you that—?

MARTIN: Don't you feel ready? Honestly now. Don't you?

JUNE: Sometimes. I guess.

MARTIN: (*Petting.*) Ummmm . . .

JUNE: But I think it's going to be worse then eating spaghetti with boys.

MARTIN: Will you forget about the damn spaghetti?

JUNE: I'm sorry.

MARTIN: Nothing to be sorry for.

(*He kisses her; she unbends a little. He is encouraged.*) That's better. Maybe I'll even teach you how to eat spaghetti someday.

JUNE: I'd like that.

(*He kisses her again.*)

Maybe I should stick with ravioli. It's easier.

MARTIN: Anybody care for kugel?

(*Another kiss; this one prolonged.*)

JUNE: Martin . . .

MARTIN: Um?

JUNE: Did you ever have a virgin?

(*An intense kiss.*)

MARTIN: You're beautiful . . .

JUNE: No, I'm not.

MARTIN: Lovely.

JUNE: Lovely maybe but not beautiful.

MARTIN: A lovely intelligent girl who reads cards and sees ghosts—and knows more about apples than anybody I ever met. And your music—

JUNE: My music?

MARTIN: You play with heart and love and warmth and I would love to love you and I'll hear the music of your body while I'm loving you.

JUNE: (*Whispering.*) All right, Martin.

(*He kisses her again with more gentle confidence. By this time they are reclining on the sofa.* MARTIN *sits up and removes his shirt and tie.* JUNE *comes out of her daze and sits up.*)

JUNE: You're not going to undress!

MARTIN: It's more fun when you're undressed.

JUNE: I don't want you to look at me!

MARTIN: You're beautiful—just remember that—you're beautiful—

JUNE: No, I'm not!

MARTIN: June, you said it was all right—

JUNE: Not if you look at me!

MARTIN: I won't look. (*He begins to open his trousers belt.*)

JUNE: Don't take off your pants!

MARTIN: June, I can't do it with my pants buttoned.

(*She looks like a frightened child about to run.*)

Okay! It's all right. See? Pants on. Nothing to worry about. Juney, nothing to worry about. . . . (*He gently embraces her and kissing her gets her down on the sofa again.*) Just a minute. (*Getting out a pack of Trojans from his pocket.*) This'll only take a second. You don't have to look.

(*He rises, back to audience.* JUNE *scrambles away. Instinctively he tries to grab her.*)

JUNE: You stay away from me! Stay away!

MARTIN: June—

JUNE: I'm not going to do it!

MARTIN: But you said—

JUNE: I don't care! I changed my mind! I can do that—I can change my mind!

MARTIN: June—shit! You've got me—

JUNE: Go away! (JUNE *is backing toward her piano which is always her refuge, clinging to it like a life raft. She is touching the keys as she has lovingly touched them earlier.*)

MARTIN: Why the hell did you lead me on?

JUNE: I was trying—I'm scared!

MARTIN: Cocktease! Bitch!

(MARTIN *slams the cover of the keyboard down on her hand, hard.* JUNE *screams. He raises the cover again.*)

Now you can't say we didn't make love, June. This is it! If you're going to play God and tell me I'm going to die—!

JUNE: I didn't—!

MARTIN: I'm going to play God too! You're never going to play the piano again! Go back to your apple graves! But don't play music! That's for people who can love—And I got your cherry the only way anybody'll ever get it.

JUNE: Please don't put that curse on me—

MARTIN: This is all you'll ever get of it, June! This!

(MARTIN *slams the keyboard cover again.* JUNE *wails.* DANIELLE, *in her slip, comes down the stairs.*)

DANIELLE: What the hell's going on down here? If you two don't shut up, my mother'll hear you all the way over on the boulevard!

MARTIN: Oh, shit! Damn it to hell—shit!

(DANIELLE *is torn between the two of them*—JUNE *sobbing and nursing her hand, and* MARTIN.)

DANIELLE: Marty—?

MARTIN: She's got me—I need a fuck! I need . . .

JUNE: Horrible! You're horrible! Dannie—help me—

DANIELLE: June—

MARTIN: She pulled the Ace of Spades! Out of that deck! She pulled the death card for me! I saw it! (*Going after* JUNE.) Witch! Obscene witch! I didn't need you to tell me I'm going to die!

DANIELLE: Come on, Marty—let her alone—

JUNE: Please—I didn't mean—

MARTIN: I'm going to die on some God damn beachhead —some cloudy beachhead—away from everybody—away from home—and Dannie—Oh, my Dannie—

DANIELLE: It's all right, Marty. Shh. It's all right. Dannie's here. Like always. Dannie's here . . . Shh. Dannie'll make it all right.

(DANIELLE, *caressing him, supporting him, takes him upstairs.* JUNE *turns and runs from the house, holding her hurt hand. She stops under the tree, looking about as though not knowing which way to run, then slowly drops to the ground in silent agony.*)

[END OF ACT TWO]

ACT THREE

It is the next morning. Lights are still on in the house, their glow foreign and in contrast to the slanting sunlight coming through the trees. JUNE is sleeping on the sofa, still wearing her party dress, but now covered with a blanket. TONY, wearing his trousers and not much else, comes down the stairs. He pauses with his hand on his stomach, looking sick. He weaves toward the kitchen and exits to re-enter almost immediately. He runs outside, leans across the porch railing, back to audience, and retches. Straightening, feeling slightly relieved, he goes inside. He sees JUNE and goes to poke her.

TONY: Hey.

JUNE: Uh—

TONY: Where's the java?

JUNE: Huh—?

TONY: I got to have some coffee. I didn't even see a coffee pot.

JUNE: (*Walking slowly.*) It's in the oven.

TONY: Oven—? You know, you people ain't normal around here.

JUNE: My mother puts it in there so she can close the lid of the stove.

TONY: Come on, get up.

JUNE: I'm—ohh—

TONY: Get the damn coffee pot out of the damn oven and make me some coffee.

JUNE: I don't know how.

TONY: What'd you mean—? You're a girl, aren't you? How come you don't know how to make coffee?

JUNE: Nobody ever showed me.

TONY: Oh, shit!—DANIELLE!

JUNE: She's not going to get up.

TONY: She's going to make me some coffee!

JUNE: If you need it so bad, why don't you go make it yourself?

TONY: I don't know how! At home they always made my coffee for me. Every morning. At home I didn't even have to ask.

JUNE: You can have some orange juice.

TONY: You know what you can do with your orange juice?—Take a douche with it!

(TONY *goes upstairs.* JUNE *has moved her hurt hand of the night before and winces. She uses this moment to inspect the hand. She moves her fingers just a little but it is obvious that the hand is injured, and throughout the act she favors it, using it only when necessary. But in this morning she is bothered by more than her hand. Her head hurts—she rubs her forehead as she looks about the room, not believing the sight of bottles and glasses and cigarette debris here. She covers her face with her good hand for a moment then goes about turning off lamps. Daylight becomes more aggressive.* TONY *comes staggering down the stairs dragging* DANIELLE *who is partially wrapped in a blanket. She is wearing her slip and has managed to grab her robe. She has been screeching all the way down, objecting.*)

TONY: I want some coffee!

DANIELLE: I don't give a damn what you want!

TONY: Now you listen here, Dannie. I mean it. I ain't like you people.

(DANIELLE, *groggy and disheveled, tries to pull herself together. She shrugs into her robe; possibly finds shoes she had kicked off the night before.*)

I don't like waking up with my buddy and me in the same bed with one girl. That is not my way. That ain't like good Christians do things.

DANIELLE: Marty was drunk—I guess he just—

TONY: I don't want to hear it!

DANIELLE: You got a dirty mind, Tony.

TONY: We were in bed together—the three of us. That's a sin. A sin against nature.

DANIELLE: Oh, go tell it to your priest.

TONY: Don't you get lippy with me! I heard a lot about good old Aunt Rose from my ex-buddy up there in my bed. And I got an idea she might like to know about what you been doing. I just might waltz over there today and open up my well-known big mouth.

DANIELLE: Come on, Tony—you've got it all wrong—

TONY: How about that coffee?

DANIELLE: Okay, okay. Then we'll talk about it, okay?

TONY: Maybe.

(DANIELLE *drags herself into the kitchen.* JUNE *has gone toward the piano, even reaching toward it, then stopping.*)

What's the matter with you?

JUNE: (*Turning from piano.*) I don't feel so good.

TONY: (*Throwing himself down and burying his face in his hands.*) No shit?

JUNE: I thought you were the clown of your outfit.

TONY: I don't feel so funny this morning.

JUNE: We have lots of toilet paper if you want to make carnations.

TONY: . . . Boy, you're just like them, ain't you? Maybe you should have come on up and joined the gang. There was room for one more in bed up there.

(JUNE *stares at him.*)

You didn't put out last night, did you? You, toots. I'm talking to you. . . . Maybe you don't remember either.

(TONY *crosses himself and gets out his rosary.* JUNE *blinks, watches for a moment, then gently—.*)

JUNE: Nothing happened. To any of us. We drank too much of all that stuff everybody brought—the beer and the wine and the whiskey—we all did. And we all got sick and nothing happened.

TONY: It happened all right. Maybe not to you but it happened. (TONY *holds his stomach as if he is feeling sick again.*)

JUNE: Can I get you anything?

(*He shakes his head.*)

That's a pretty rosary. The beads—

TONY: My sister Maria gave it to me—she's got one just like it. Maria and me. . . . You want to be a nun or something?

JUNE: There are no Evangelical nuns.

TONY: Maybe there ought to be.

JUNE: Yes. Maybe.

TONY: In my family we got a priest and two nuns. When Maria goes into the convent it'll be three. They're good people.

JUNE: I'm sure they are.

TONY: If they ever find out about this—!

JUNE: Nobody'll tell, Tony. You can pretend you never came here.

(MARTY *comes down the stairs, weakly, sickly.* TONY *looks at him, then rises and goes into the kitchen.* MARTY *is much the worse for wear. He has put on his pants and drags his shirt. He blinks into the light after* TONY.)

MARTIN: What's the matter with him?

JUNE: I don't think he liked waking up three in a bed.

MARTIN: (*Sinking into a chair.*) I feel like the top of my head's coming off.

JUNE: I feel like the fingers of my hand are coming off.

MARTIN: Oh. That really happened, didn't it? Are they broken?

JUNE: My whole hand throbs.

MARTIN: Can you move your fingers?

JUNE: A little.

MARTIN: That means they're not broken. I think.

JUNE: I get so tired sometimes. . . . It's like going around wearing lead shoes.

MARTIN: I threw up all over your mother's bathroom.

JUNE: Ohhh.

MARTIN: Oh . . . God . . .

JUNE: Are you going to be sick again?

MARTIN: We're supposed to go over to Aunt Rose's today—she'll be hugging me—like a son come home from the war—I can't do it! I can't go over there!

JUNE: Well, you can't stay here—it's going to take me hours to clean up this place. I don't even know if I can. My hand's hurt and my stomach's . . . I feel like I'm dying.

(JUNE *immediately wishes she hadn't said that but* MARTIN'S *reaction is dazed.*)

MARTIN: My father was in World War I . . .

JUNE: What—?

MARTIN: He says the French—they call sex the Little Death . . .

(MARTIN *begins to chant the mourner's Kaddish softly, to himself.* JUNE *looks at him, then goes to the kitchen door.*)

JUNE: Dannie—?

(DANIELLE *enters from the kitchen.*)

DANIELLE: That coffee's not doing Tony much good. He's sick.

JUNE: Look at Marty. Dannie, how are we going to get them out of here?

DANIELLE: Don't worry—

JUNE: It'll take hours just to clean up this room—

DANIELLE: It's not that bad.

JUNE: Why is he doing that?

DANIELLE: Marty—?

MARTIN: (*Recoiling from her.*) Don't touch me! . . . There's a ritual of purification for women . . . After the menses they go into the water and come out pure. I wish they had a purification ritual for men . . .

DANIELLE: (*Angrily.*) If you want to get clean, there's a bathtub upstairs!

MARTIN: It wouldn't help.

DANIELLE: Do you want some coffee, Martin?

MARTIN: You give everything to dying soldiers, don't you?

JUNE: I'm going to take aspirin. Maybe that'll help. (JUNE *goes up stairs.*)

DANIELLE: June—! Aspirin'll only make her sick. (*She looks at* MARTIN *who is cradling his face in his hands; she goes to open the front door.*) Come on, Marty—get some fresh air. Stand on the porch and breathe deep—that's what Morey always does. Come. You'll feel better. Come.

(*She goes outside;* MARTIN *rises as if he cannot help himself and slowly follows her outside. She moves out under the tree where the shifting shadows of morning sunlight move around her.* MARTIN *stands on the porch.*)

MARTIN: Dannie . . . You look—in that little robe—you look like you're—thirteen. And just come back to Seattle for the summer . . . you came from the station in the morning —beautiful dark child—but I was a man. I couldn't play with you—even when you brought the morning into that house. It was a dark house before you came, Dannie . . .

never enough light. The candles Mother lit on Friday— they couldn't light up those rooms. We all loved you. My family. Did you know that? But I loved you most. If, my father hadn't found out—if he hadn't seen letters I was writing—if he hadn't watched us—if he hadn't made me understand that you were in our home as a sister . . . (MARTIN, *drawn by her, to her, goes into the yard.*)

DANIELLE: If he hadn't—?

(MARTIN *comes close; light becomes stronger; the spell breaks. He turns and runs into the house to grab his shirt and put it on.* DANIELLE *comes into the house.*)

MARTIN: I'm going back to camp.

DANIELLE: What about my mother?

MARTIN: Tell her my leave was cancelled!

DANIELLE: What about Tony?

MARTIN: Let him go back to Philadelphia.

DANIELLE: Marty, is it that bad? What we did last night—is it that bad?

MARTIN: You don't understand! You never will! Things that twisted me up and made me sick—you always could laugh at. Even my father! Even my father . . .

DANIELLE: No, I don't understand you, Martin. By God, that's true. Like you said, when I was in Seattle every time I turned around I fell over you! Since I was ten years old. So finally last night you got up the nerve to do what your father stopped you from doing then.

MARTIN: You're my cousin!

DANIELLE: That's not a taboo!

MARTIN: In our home it was!

DANIELLE: Marty, you're not a little kid asking the questions at Seder any more. You are out of that dark house. You are a soldier!

MARTIN: And you'd do as much for any soldier, wouldn't you?

DANIELLE: I'd do more for you, Marty.

MARTIN: Send me off to die with a clean shirt and a cup of coffee. That's what women do, isn't it? Set up canteens and give us doughnuts so there's something in our gut when we're shot.

DANIELLE: Marty. You listen to me. Okay, June pulled the Ace of Spades when she told your cards. You want to know how serious I take that? She told my cat's fortune four years ago and she pulled the Ace of Spades for the cat. But my cat didn't die. As a matter of fact, she had kittens two weeks later and she's still going strong. It's a game—June's cards are a game. You're not going to die, Marty. You're going to be a hero and you're going to come back after the war. Home. To—us. That's my prediction. And it's just as good as hers. Marty, you're just scared—

MARTIN: Yeah. I am. That's why I wanted this weekend. . . . See, like a weekend where you take pictures of everybody with their arms around each other, sitting on Aunt Rose's front porch, and you put them in your wallet in those little cellophane cases and you take them out when you're sitting in strange places where nobody knows you and you look at them and you say, "Yeah, this is what I carry with me. This."

DANIELLE: Oh, Marty—

(JUNE *comes miserably down the stairs. She has begun to clean up and carries any clothing which have been discarded up there.* MARTIN *has pulled into himself again.*)

June, what am I going to do? Marty's—I don't know—he says he's not going to my mother's today. He says he's going back to camp.

JUNE: Maybe he should.

DANIELLE: Oh, you don't care what happens to us, do you?

JUNE: Yes, but—

DANIELLE: No! You just want to get us out of here so you can clean up for your precious mother. Look at him! If you hadn't told his cards he wouldn't be this way.

JUNE: It wasn't the cards—

DANIELLE: It was! It was! Your mother's right—the cards are evil!

JUNE: I need them!

DANIELLE: So you can tell people they're going to die? (*Going to kitchen door.*) Tony!

(TONY *enters, sees his shirt which* JUNE *has brought down, and puts it on.*)

You know what this nut wants to do? He says he's going back to camp. Tell him. Tell him he can't go.

TONY: What do I care what he does?

DANIELLE: He's your buddy!

TONY: Some buddy.

DANIELLE: So he was sick and I put him to bed! With us. So what? I couldn't carry him, could I? He just fell into the bed and I couldn't move him—he was sick. I was too. Like you. I just—passed out.

TONY: Is that the truth?

DANIELLE: Ask June if you don't believe me.

TONY: She wasn't there.

DANIELLE: She saw me when I came downstairs to get Marty. Didn't you, June?

JUNE: I already told him. I told him nothing happened.

TONY: I don't know—

JUNE: They could hardly even get up the steps. Dannie's a drum majorette and all that goes with it but you don't think she'd do a thing like that, do you?

TONY: (*Hopefully.*) Well—

DANIELLE: That's right, Tony. So we got blotto. So what? Come on—talk to this goose. Don't let him bust up the weekend.

TONY: Marty, maybe we could—

MARTIN: Oh, go home to Philadelphia.

TONY: I don't want to go home to Philadelphia! I said good-bye down there. What'm I supposed to do? Get everybody crying again? Jesus. You know why I had to go to the men's room in such a hurry there at the station? So they wouldn't see me cry, that's why. Shit. What a shit leave. Maybe it'd be better if we do go back to camp and get it over with.

(*Outside, in the yard,* WALLY *and* LORRAINE *enter.* WALLY *is angry;* LORRAINE *looks forlorn.*)

DANIELLE: No! Marty, tell him to stay! Tell him nothing happened.

MARTIN: Your're a liar.

DANIELLE: You're another! (*Going to* TONY.) Tony, if he's going to act like that, why don't you come to my house? Just like we planned. My mother makes great blintzes. She's been cooking for a week. For soldiers. You come—you come.

(WALLY *and* LORRAINE *walk into the house. The moment after is silent. Everybody stares.* LORRAINE *is first to break. Putting her handkerchief over her mouth and nose, she runs upstairs.*)

WALLY: What the hell—

DANIELLE: Mr. Eisenhart! You know my cousin Martin, don't you? He's spending some of his leave at our house—with his buddy, Tony here. His buddy. They're both stay-ing at my house. We thought—today—it's still warm enough for a picnic. June—I guess you don't want to go now—on the picnic. So maybe we'd better—

WALLY: What's been going on in this house?

DANIELLE: Nothing!

WALLY: June, what's been going on here?

JUNE: Nothing—nothing!

TONY: We just came over here this morning to—

WALLY: This morning! You did all this in one morning? How damn dumb do you think I am?

JUNE: No, they were here last night, too! Last night. But they came back again—

TONY: Sure did. For the picnic. Dannie's my girl. Dannie here. Hardly know June over there. No, sir—

WALLY: (*At* MARTIN.) You look a little sick. I'd be sick too if I got caught with my pants down.

JUNE: Please! Let him alone!

WALLY: What've you done to my daughter? You kids today —coming right into a man's home! In my day, if a fellow was going to screw a girl he didn't do it right in her father's house!

(MARTIN *rises, faces them for a brief moment, then turns and runs out of the house to exit through the yard.*)

Hey, you! If you've got my daughter knocked up I'll get you no matter how far you run! Scum is easy to find!

(WALLY *has followed* MARTIN *onto the porch then turns and goes into the room to grab* TONY *who is trying to finish dressing.* WALLY *propels him to the door.*)

You get the hell out of my house! Go after your buddy, mister! (*He then turns on* DANIELLE *who has gone protectively to* JUNE.)

WALLY: You little slut—go on! Get out! Go with your punks! And don't you ever come back! No daughter of mine is going to run with whores!

DANIELLE: (*With courage.*) June—?

JUNE: I'm okay. Go on. Take care of them—Marty. Maybe if you talk to him. Now. Maybe he will go home with you. I'll call. I'll call you. Later.

(DANIELLE *runs from the house, joins* TONY, *and they exit together, after* MARTIN.)

Dad—

WALLY: (*Shoving her roughly toward the party debris.*) You clean up that mess! I hope you flushed the toilet twice so the rubbers went down because if that crazy mother of yours sees anything like that she'll go all the way nuts.

JUNE: You've done worse!

(WALLY *slaps her across the face.*)

A lot worse!

WALLY: Now I know why you talked your mother into going away this weekend! So you could have your punk boyfriend over here. I should have guessed but I'm a little thick sometimes. I didn't think Junebaby was interested in anything but the tony music she plays.

JUNE: You're wrong. I didn't do anything.

WALLY: Well, if that's true, you're even more of a cripple than I thought. (*Picking up the flask; taking a drink himself.*) So all this didn't help, huh? What's the matter? A chip off the old block of ice like your mother, huh?

JUNE: Stop it!

WALLY: God. Jesusgod. It takes a saint to live with you two! And I'm no saint. (*More calm.*) Go on. Clean up before she comes down again. I don't know how she's going to take this on top of all the other.

JUNE: (*Slowly picking up some debris.*) What happened?

WALLY: What the hell do you think happened?

JUNE: You didn't stay for the thing. The dedication.

WALLY: I should never have gone. But good-hearted Wally took it laying down again. Trying to make something out of this family—

JUNE: *What happened?*

WALLY: She sat there on that damned train for three hours with a handkerchief over her face—

JUNE: Well, if that was all—

WALLY: Then, after we got there, everybody was hungry so we went out to eat. But she wouldn't go inside the restaurant with the rest of us. Oh, no. Said she didn't eat in restaurants like rich people. So while we went in to order a meal she stood right outside the restaurant window like some—beggar —with a bag of potato chips.

JUNE: She loves potato chips.

WALLY: I feel like slapping your mouth again. You know that? So often I just want to lay one on you. Knock your teeth down your damn mealy-mouthed throat.

(JUNE *puts a piece of furniture between herself and* WALLY. *Instead of physically striking her, he leans forward to spit words at her.*)

WALLY: Stu Whittaker asked me if I was too cheap to buy the wife a meal. God. I just grabbed a sandwich and got the hell out of there. Only my old buddy Stu follows us—all the way back to the hotel. Drunk as the Lord—talking to her. Asking her where she got those stupid flowers she was wearing. Said he wanted to get some for his girlfriend. You know what he does when we get to the lobby of the hotel? Asks us to come along in the bar for a drink. And what was so crazy about it, she said, "Okay." Like she was mesmerized by him or something. Stu is going to spike her drink—I knew it. He goes over to the bar, so I gets up and follows. Sure enough, Stu was having the bartender put gin in her 7-Up. I tried to stop him and . . . Well, it just got out of hand. He slugged me. Stu Whittaker slugged me . . . I was in the Argonne with Stu and he slugged me! Then I pasted him up against the bar—we must have broke a hundred glasses before they threw us out.

JUNE: It wasn't her fault! It was Stu Whittaker's.

WALLY: She could have said "No!"

JUNE: So could you! You could have gone right up to your room instead of—

WALLY: Oh, yeah! Where we were supposed to have our second honeymoon. Isn't that what you hollered after us? Second honeymoon!

(*She tries to evade him but he blocks her, talking into her face.*)

I'm going to tell you all about our second honeymoon because I want you to understand. I don't expect you to understand but I'm going to try to reach you just once more.

JUNE: When did you ever try before?

WALLY: You—damn! We hadn't been together in a bedroom for—shit. Ten years. And you know what she does? Get blankets off the bed and a pillow and puts them on the floor. She was going to lay down on the crummy floor of that hotel room rather then get in bed aside of me. Hell, I wouldn't have touched her. You can bet I told her a few of the facts of life she never wants to talk about.

JUNE: Oh, no.

WALLY: Then I dragged her the hell out of there and brought her back to—this. And she hasn't said one word since we left that hotel. After this mess she won't talk for a month! See? See what you did to her?

JUNE: I was only trying to help.

WALLY: You think your shit's ice cream, don't you? *You're* going to help? Us? There is no help—and sure not anything *you* could give.

JUNE: *Dad*—!

WALLY: What do you know about what we went through, huh? She was only my wife for a year before she got sick. One crappy year I had a real wife. And you're going to help? Even the doctors couldn't help. Rest homes. Operations. Nothing's helped. Those damn doctors don't know anything about women. (*Taking another drink from* MARTIN'S *flask.*) That woman is falling away . . . This is your fault! You did this. Why didn't you go out someplace if you wanted to shack up with some soldier this weekend? Why'd you have to get us in on it? Doing it in front of your mother like this—probably in her own bed! Well, all I can say is I hope it was worth it. I hope you found out what people do in bed. Normal people. What happens when they do it. . . . What happened when I did it with her was you and a dead boy.

JUNE: I didn't ask to be born!

WALLY: Well, I didn't ask for you to be born either! I mean, what is it? A life sentence?

JUNE: Dad, maybe if you—

WALLY: Yeah. Maybe. Maybe a lot of things.

(WALLY *grabs his hat and goes into the yard.* JUNE *follows.*)

JUNE: Where're you going?

WALLY: Downtown. And I don't know when or if I'll be back.

JUNE: Dad!

WALLY: I'm not doing anybody here any good. Why should I crucify myself? If you're old enough to spend the weekend picking up soldiers, June, you're old enough for me to get out from under.

JUNE: We need you!

WALLY: I'll send money.

JUNE: I'll run away! I'll go to New York City and be an actress. And I won't come back! I won't help her!

WALLY: Oh, June. You're not going anywhere. Your brain's like mush. Like hers. Neither one of you can even wring a chicken's neck.

JUNE: I'll show you!

WALLY: I won't be watching.

JUNE: I know about Margey! I'm going to tell Mother about Margey! If you don't come right back here, she can get a lawyer! Adulterer! She can charge you with that! We can take away all your money and—the secondhand welding machines! Everything!

WALLY: Get out of my life!

(WALLY *exits without looking back.* JUNE *calls after him.*)

JUNE: I've never been in your life. *Her*—*she*—that's what you called me—and it came out of your mouth like dirty words. Listen to me! Dad, listen to me—talk to me!

(*Out on the street there is the sound of an automobile starting up and deliberately, almost calmly, taking off. Inside the house,* LORRAINE *has come downstairs. She has removed her go-away clothes and wears a dark housecoat with a sweater. She wanders out of the house and goes to the apple tree.*)

LORRAINE: I don't remember where I went or what I did or when I came back. Some days—it's so hard to wake up in the morning after being dead all night.

(JUNE *goes to her mother.*)

Don't you touch me! Don't you come near me!

(*She has pulled away from* JUNE *and now climbs into the tree and sits on a lower limb.*)

You're dirty now.

JUNE: What're you doing—?

LORRAINE: Going up to where it's quiet. Nobody shouts at you when you're sitting in a tree.

JUNE: I'll shout at you if you stay up there.

(LORRAINE *picks an apple and throws it at* JUNE.)

Cut it out!

LORRAINE: All sorts of things fall out of trees, don't they? . . . Blossoms—and the feathers of birds—apples— and finally—leaves.

JUNE: Mother, Dad's gone downtown.

LORRAINE: I like the way old orchards breathe. The blossoms in the spring and the sour smell of apples in fall.

JUNE: He might not be coming back here. He said he was going to stay away.

LORRAINE: When I was a little girl on the farm in Indiana—I had a big tree just like this I could climb—in the orchard. Where my father had buried all my mother's miscarriages. Sometimes I think we should have buried her there too—near the little babies. But maybe she wouldn't have liked that. Maybe—I'm the one should be buried there.

JUNE: Did you hear what I just said?

LORRAINE: Oh. Yes.

JUNE: Mother. Please come down.

LORRAINE: No. I'm not ever coming down. It's dirty down there.

JUNE: Mother, listen—you're going to forget all about last night—yesterday—and this morning. I'm going to clean up the house and then we're going to forget all about it, okay? You come on down now and we'll pretend we slept through the weekend. Wasn't it silly of us to sleep so long?

LORRAINE: I can't walk down there. There are rotten apples all over the ground.

JUNE: Suppose I leave too? (*Moving away.*) Suppose I walk away right now and let you alone up in that tree?

LORRAINE: June! Come here.

(JUNE *stops.*)

Up here. With me.

JUNE: I can't. I hurt my hand. You can't climb trees with a hurt hand.

LORRAINE: But I have to tell you something.

JUNE: You can tell me. You can talk to me even if I'm not up there with you.

LORRAINE: . . . Don't be like me, June. That's all I wanted to say.

JUNE: He says I am. He said that.

LORRAINE: What does he know? Oh, June—what does anybody know?

JUNE: One thing I know—I'm going inside now and clean the house. When you get tired of sitting up there, climb down again.

LORRAINE: I won't.

JUNE: Yes, you will. Even if it is dirty down here. And I'll tell you why. Nobody stays in one place forever. Sooner or later, Mother—sooner or later. You have to move.

(JUNE *goes into the house. She looks at the piano then, with finality, closes the cover over the keys and begins to pick up debris, putting bottles and other things into a waste can. She gets her cards, holds them to her for a moment, then drops them into the waste can with the other debris as lights fade to dark.*)

[END OF PLAY]

One Acts ~ And ~ Monologues ~ For ~

Women

BY ~ LUDMILLA BOLLOW

These haunting plays mark the arrival of a new voice in the American Theater. This volume consists of two thirty to thirty-five minute monologues and a forty minute one-act for two women. All three call for simple interior sets.

This delightful small scale musical is about the life of Gilbert and Sullivan. It is interspersed with some of the best known songs from the Savoy operas, including THE PIRATES OF PENZANCE, HMS PINAFORE and THE MIKADO. This show had a very successful run on the West End of London in 1975. Five males, three females, though more actors may be used as "stage-hands" and chorus members. Settings may be fluid and simple, or complex. A piano vocal score is available for perusal or rental.

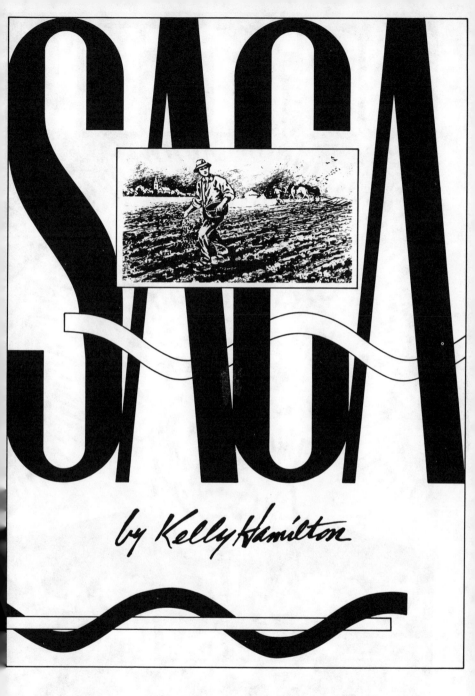

SAGA

by Kelly Hamilton

This wonderful musical is a history of America's pioneers as they push their way across the country. A minimum of eight males and eight females are necessary, and the show can be expanded to use many more actors. Settings can be fluid and simple or elaborate. A piano vocal score is available for perusal or rental.

BATTERY

BY DANIEL THERRIAULT

Electricity is the central metaphor and an expressive image for this unusual love story set in an electrical workshop. This young playwright has been compared to Sam Shepard and David Mamet for his superb use of language. Two males, one female; single interior set.

LOOKING-GLASS

by Michael Sutton and Cynthia Mandelberg

This provocative chronicle, interspersed with fantasy sequences from ALICE IN WONDERLAND, traces the career of Charles Dodgson (better known as Lewis Carroll) from his first work on the immortal classic, to his near downfall when accused of immorality. Six males, four females with some doubling; either simple fluid staging or elaborate sets can be used.

SOME RAIN

by James Edward Luczak

Set in rural Alabama in 1968, the play is a bittersweet tale of a middle-aged waitress whose ability to love and be loved is re-kindled by her chance encounter with a young drifter. Two males, one female; single interior and exterior set.

DEATH in the POT

by Manuel Van Loggem

An English style thriller with a fascinating plot that takes intricate twists and turns, as a husband and wife try to kill each other off, aided by a mysterious Merchant of Death. Four males, two females; single interior set.

A musical presentation of magical and possible events in the lives of two women born in the last century. A minimum of three males and four females, though it can be expanded to accommodate a great number; may be done with simple fluid staging. A piano vocal score is available for perusal or rental.

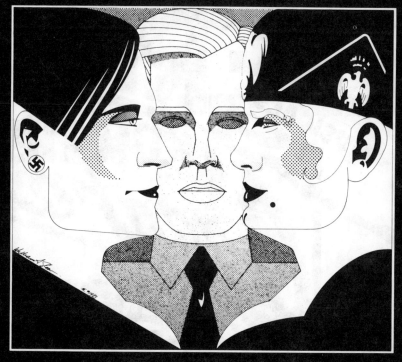

ROBERT DAVID MacDONALD

Set in the Berlin chancellery in 1941, this play is a fictional encounter between the mistresses of Hitler and Mussolini: Eva Braun and Clara Petacci. This show had a successful run on London's West End in 1982 with Glenda Jackson. There are some restrictions on production rights.

HIGH ENERGY MUSICALS FROM THE *Omaha* MAGIC THEATER

This volume contains three of the dynamic shows created by members of the Omaha Magic Theatre: **Megan Terry**, Jo Ann Schmidman, Marianne de Pury, Lynn Herrick and John J. Sheehan. AMERICAN KING'S ENGLISH FOR QUEENS, RUNNING GAG, BABES IN THE BIGHOUSE are all shows that call for more females than males, and have simple flexible sets.

ESCOFFIER, KING OF CHEFS
by
Owen S. Rackleff

In this one-man show set in a Monte Carlo villa at the end of the last century, the grand master of the kitchen, Escoffier, ponders a glorious return from retirement. In doing so, he relates anecdotes about the famous and shares his mouth-watering recipes with the audience. One male; single interior set.

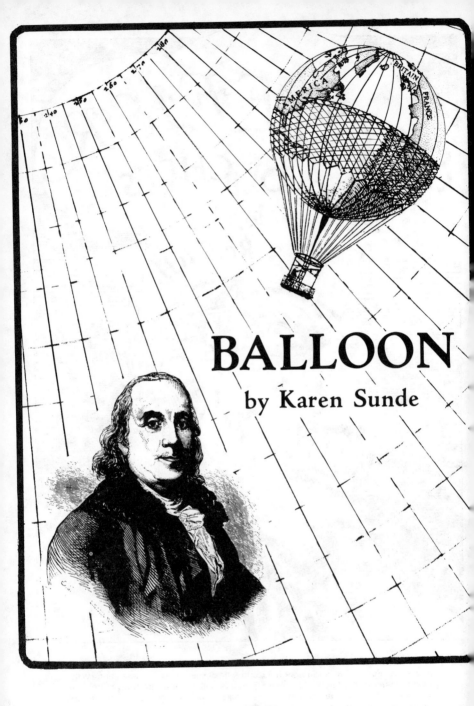

BALLOON

by Karen Sunde

18th century Paris is the setting of this structurally inventive play about Benjamin Franklin and his French contemporaries. Five males, one female; single interior set.

A charming musical adaptation of Shakespeare's A MIDSUMMER NIGHT'S DREAM.
This is one of the three shows written by the man who gave us LITTLE MARY
SUNSHINE. Five males, three females, expandable with the use of a chorus; single
exterior set. A piano score is available for perusal or rental.

This gem of a play evokes the **days of youth and innocence** as our boys were being shipped off to World War II. The casting calls for three males and three females, and there are some excellent scenes for two women.

ISBN: 0-88145-18-